The Ultimate Pla
Mediterranean Cookbook
For Beginners

365 Days of Easy, Mouthwatering, and Nutrient-Rich Recipes with 30-Day Meal Plan to Boost Your Immune System

Francesca Munro

Table of Contents

Introduction

The Mediterranean diet is a way of eating based on the traditional cuisine of countries surrounding the Mediterranean Sea, such as Greece, Italy, and Spain. This diet is characterized by a high consumption of plant-based foods, whole grains, and healthy fats, along with moderate amounts of fish and dairy, and limited intake of red meat and sweets.

Benefits of a Mediterranean Diet

Numerous studies have shown that following a Mediterranean diet can have numerous health benefits, including:

Reduced risk of heart disease: The Mediterranean diet is rich in heart-healthy monounsaturated and polyunsaturated fats, which can help lower cholesterol levels and reduce the risk of heart disease.

Improved brain function: Research suggests that the Mediterranean diet may help improve cognitive function and reduce the risk of Alzheimer's disease and other forms of dementia.

Lowered risk of cancer: A Mediterranean diet rich in fruits, vegetables, and whole grains has been associated with a reduced risk of certain types of cancer, including breast, colon, and prostate cancer.

Better weight management: The Mediterranean diet is naturally low in calories and high in fiber, which can help with weight loss and weight management.

Vegetarianism and the Mediterranean Diet

While the Mediterranean diet does include moderate amounts of fish and dairy, it is still possible to follow a vegetarian or even a vegan version of this diet. Plant-based sources of protein, such as legumes, nuts, and seeds, are a staple in the Mediterranean diet, making it easy to create delicious and nutritious vegetarian meals.

Some vegetarian Mediterranean diet staples include:

Hummus: Made from chickpeas, tahini, lemon juice, and garlic, hummus is a nutritious and versatile dip that can be enjoyed with vegetables or whole grain pita bread.

Falafel: These fried or baked balls made from ground chickpeas or fava beans are a staple of Mediterranean cuisine and can be served in sandwiches, salads, or as a snack.

Spanakopita: A Greek dish made with spinach and feta cheese wrapped in phyllo dough, spanakopita can be served as a main dish or as an appetizer.

Caponata: A Sicilian dish made with eggplant, tomatoes, olives, and capers, caponata can be enjoyed as a side dish or as a topping for whole grain pasta or bread.

Overall, a Mediterranean diet that emphasizes plant-based foods and healthy fats can be a delicious and nutritious way to support your health and well-being, whether you are a vegetarian or not.

Section 1: Appetizers and Small Bites

Hummus with Pita Chips

Ingredients:

- 2 cans chickpeas, drained and rinsed
- 2 cloves garlic, minced
- 1/4 cup tahini
- 1/4 cup lemon juice
- 1/4 cup olive oil
- 1 teaspoon ground cumin
- Salt and pepper, to taste
- Pita chips, for serving

Instructions:

1. In a food processor, pulse the chickpeas until they are broken down and form a rough paste.
2. Add the garlic, tahini, lemon juice, olive oil, cumin, salt, and pepper to the food processor and blend until smooth.
3. Taste the hummus and adjust the seasoning as needed.
4. Transfer the hummus to a serving bowl and drizzle with a little bit of olive oil.
5. Serve with pita chips for dipping.

Baba Ghanoush with Crudités

Ingredients:
- 2 large eggplants
- 2 cloves garlic, minced

- 1/4 cup tahini
- 1/4 cup lemon juice
- 1/4 cup olive oil
- Salt and pepper, to taste
- Assorted raw vegetables (such as carrots, cucumbers, and cherry tomatoes), for serving.

Instructions:

1. Preheat the oven to 400°F.
2. Prick the eggplants all over with a fork and place them on a baking sheet. Roast in the oven for 30-40 minutes, or until the eggplants are completely soft and the skin is charred.
3. Let the eggplants cool for a few minutes, then slice them in half

lengthwise and scoop out the flesh with a spoon.

4. Place the eggplant flesh in a food processor and add the garlic, tahini, lemon juice, olive oil, salt, and pepper. Blend until smooth.

5. Taste the baba ghanoush and adjust the seasoning as needed.

6. Transfer the baba ghanoush to a serving bowl and drizzle with a little bit of olive oil.

7. Serve with raw vegetables for dipping.

Spanakopita (Greek Spinach Pie)

Ingredients:

- 1/2 cup olive oil
- 1 onion, finely chopped

- 2 cloves garlic, minced
- 1 pound fresh spinach, washed and chopped
- 1/4 cup chopped fresh parsley
- 1/4 cup chopped fresh dill
- 1/4 cup crumbled feta cheese
- Salt and pepper, to taste
- 1 package phyllo dough
- 1/2 cup melted butter

Instructions:

1. Preheat the oven to 375°F.
2. Heat the olive oil in a large skillet over medium heat. Add the onion and garlic and sauté until soft and fragrant, about 5 minutes.
3. Add the spinach to the skillet and sauté until wilted and tender, about 5-7 minutes.

4. Remove the skillet from the heat and stir in the parsley, dill, feta cheese, salt, and pepper.

5. Lay out a sheet of phyllo dough and brush it with melted butter. Lay another sheet of phyllo dough on top and brush it with butter. Repeat until you have used half of the phyllo sheets.

6. Spoon the spinach mixture onto the phyllo dough, spreading it out evenly.

7. Layer the remaining phyllo sheets on top of the spinach mixture, brushing each sheet with butter as you go.

8. Brush the top layer of phyllo with butter and sprinkle with a little bit of water.

9. Use a sharp knife to cut the spanakopita into pieces, making sure to cut all the way through the phyllo layers.

10. Bake the spanakopita in the preheated oven for 30-40 minutes, or until golden brown and crispy on top.

11. Let the spanakopita cool for a few minutes, then slice and serve warm.

Note: Spanakopita can be made ahead of time and reheated in the oven before serving. Leftovers can be stored in the refrigerator and reheated in the oven or microwave.

Falafel with Tzatziki Sauce

Ingredients:

- 2 cups dried chickpeas, soaked overnight
- 1 onion, roughly chopped
- 4 garlic cloves, chopped
- 1/4 cup chopped fresh parsley
- 1/4 cup chopped fresh cilantro
- 1 tablespoon ground cumin
- 1 tablespoon ground coriander
- 1 teaspoon salt
- 1/2 teaspoon black pepper
- 1/2 teaspoon baking soda
- 1/4 cup all-purpose flour
- Vegetable oil, for frying
- Pita bread, for serving
- Tzatziki sauce, for serving

Instructions:

1. Drain the soaked chickpeas and rinse them with cold water. Pat them dry with a paper towel and place them in a food processor.

2. Add the onion, garlic, parsley, cilantro, cumin, coriander, salt, black pepper, and baking soda to the food processor. Pulse until the mixture is finely ground but not pureed.

3. Transfer the mixture to a bowl and stir in the flour. The mixture should hold together when squeezed in your hand. If it's too dry, add a little water; if it's too wet, add a little more flour.

4. Heat the vegetable oil in a large saucepan over medium-high heat.

5. Using your hands, shape the mixture into small balls, about 1 1/2 inches in diameter. Place them on a plate or tray.

6. Once the oil is hot, carefully add the falafel balls to the pan in batches. Fry until golden brown and crispy, about 3-5 minutes per batch.

7. Using a slotted spoon, transfer the falafel balls to a paper towel-lined plate to drain excess oil.

8. Serve the falafel with pita bread and tzatziki sauce on the side.

Stuffed Grape Leaves (Dolmades)

Ingredients:

- 1 jar grape leaves, drained and rinsed
- 1 cup white rice
- 1 onion, finely chopped
- 1/4 cup chopped fresh parsley
- 1/4 cup chopped fresh dill
- 1/4 cup chopped fresh mint
- 1/4 cup lemon juice
- 1/4 cup olive oil
- Salt and black pepper, to taste
- Water

Instructions:

1. In a large bowl, combine the rice, onion, parsley, dill, mint, lemon juice, olive oil, salt, and black pepper. Mix well.
2. To stuff the grape leaves, lay a leaf flat on a work surface with the

shiny side down and the stem end facing you. Place a spoonful of the rice mixture near the stem end of the leaf.

3. Fold the stem end over the filling, then fold in the sides of the leaf and roll it up tightly.

4. Repeat with the remaining grape leaves and filling.

5. Place the stuffed grape leaves in a large pot, arranging them in a single layer.

6. Add enough water to the pot to cover the grape leaves.

7. Bring the water to a boil, then reduce the heat to low and cover the pot with a lid.

8. Simmer the stuffed grape leaves for 30-40 minutes, or until the rice

is cooked through and the grape leaves are tender.

9. Serve the dolmades warm or at room temperature.

Roasted Red Pepper and Feta Dip

Ingredients:

- 2 red bell peppers, roasted and peeled
- 1/2 cup crumbled feta cheese
- 1/2 cup Greek yogurt
- 1 garlic clove, minced
- 1/4 teaspoon paprika
- 1/4 teaspoon dried oregano
- Salt and black pepper, to taste
- Olive oil, for drizzling

Instructions:

1. Preheat the oven to 400°F (200°C).

2. Place the red bell peppers on a baking sheet and roast in the oven for 20-25 minutes, or until the skin is charred and blistered.

3. Remove the peppers from the oven and let them cool. Once cool enough to handle, peel off the skin and remove the seeds and stem.

4. In a food processor, combine the roasted peppers, feta cheese, Greek yogurt, minced garlic, paprika, dried oregano, salt, and black pepper. Process until the mixture is smooth and creamy.

5. Transfer the dip to a bowl and drizzle with olive oil.

6. Serve the dip with pita bread or crackers.

Mediterranean Bruschetta with Tomatoes, Olives, and Feta

Ingredients:

- 4 large tomatoes, diced
- 1/2 cup pitted Kalamata olives, chopped
- 1/2 cup crumbled feta cheese
- 2 garlic cloves, minced
- 2 tablespoons chopped fresh basil
- 1 tablespoon chopped fresh oregano
- 1 tablespoon balsamic vinegar
- Salt and black pepper, to taste
- Baguette, sliced

Instructions:

1. In a bowl, combine the diced tomatoes, chopped Kalamata olives, crumbled feta cheese, minced garlic, chopped fresh basil, chopped fresh oregano, balsamic vinegar, salt, and black pepper. Mix well.

2. Preheat the oven to 375°F (190°C).

3. Arrange the sliced baguette on a baking sheet and bake in the oven for 5-7 minutes, or until the bread is lightly toasted.

4. Remove the bread from the oven and let it cool for a minute.

5. Top each slice of bread with a spoonful of the tomato and olive mixture.

6. Serve the bruschetta immediately.

Fried Zucchini Fritters with Mint Yogurt Sauce

Ingredients:

- 2 medium-sized zucchinis
- 1/2 cup of all-purpose flour
- 1/2 teaspoon of baking powder
- 1/2 teaspoon of salt
- 1/4 teaspoon of black pepper
- 1/4 teaspoon of dried oregano
- 1/4 teaspoon of dried basil
- 2 eggs
- 1/4 cup of milk
- 1/4 cup of chopped fresh mint
- 1/2 cup of plain yogurt
- Vegetable oil for frying

Instructions:

1. Grate the zucchinis and place them in a bowl. Sprinkle with salt and let them sit for 10 minutes to release some moisture.

2. Squeeze out the excess liquid from the zucchini with your hands and discard it.

3. In a separate bowl, mix together the flour, baking powder, salt, black pepper, oregano, and basil.

4. In another bowl, beat the eggs and add the milk. Stir in the grated zucchini and then the dry ingredients.

5. Heat the vegetable oil in a frying pan over medium-high heat.

6. Drop spoonfuls of the zucchini mixture into the hot oil and fry until golden brown, flipping once.

7. Drain the fritters on a paper towel-lined plate.
8. In a small bowl, mix together the chopped mint and plain yogurt.
9. Serve the fried zucchini fritters with the mint yogurt sauce on the side.

Eggplant Caponata

Ingredients:

- 1 medium-sized eggplant, diced
- 1/2 red onion, diced
- 1 stalk of celery, diced
- 1/4 cup of diced green olives
- 2 tablespoons of capers
- 1/2 cup of diced canned tomatoes
- 1 tablespoon of red wine vinegar
- 1 tablespoon of honey

- 2 tablespoons of chopped fresh parsley
- 2 tablespoons of olive oil
- Salt and black pepper to taste

Instructions:

1. Heat the olive oil in a large skillet over medium-high heat.
2. Add the diced eggplant and sauté for 5-7 minutes, until browned.
3. Add the diced onion and celery and sauté for another 3-4 minutes, until softened.
4. Add the diced green olives, capers, canned tomatoes, red wine vinegar, and honey.
5. Reduce the heat to low and simmer for 10-15 minutes, stirring occasionally, until the eggplant is

tender and the mixture is thickened.

6. Season with salt and black pepper to taste.

7. Stir in the chopped parsley and let cool to room temperature before serving.

Fava Bean Puree with Cumin and Lemon

Ingredients:

- 2 cups of shelled fava beans
- 1/4 cup of tahini
- 1/4 cup of lemon juice
- 1/4 cup of water
- 2 cloves of garlic, minced
- 1/2 teaspoon of ground cumin
- Salt and black pepper to taste

- 2 tablespoons of olive oil
- 1 tablespoon of chopped fresh parsley

Instructions:

1. Bring a pot of salted water to a boil and blanch the fava beans for 2-3 minutes, until tender.
2. Drain the fava beans and rinse under cold water to cool them down.
3. Remove the outer skin from the fava beans by squeezing them gently.
4. In a food processor, combine the fava beans, tahini, lemon juice, water, minced garlic, ground cumin, salt and black pepper to taste.

5. Process the mixture until smooth and creamy, scraping down the sides of the bowl as needed.

6.

7. Drizzle in the olive oil and pulse a few times to combine.

8. Transfer the fava bean puree to a serving bowl and garnish with chopped parsley.

9. Serve the puree with pita bread or sliced vegetables for dipping.

Greek Salad Skewers with Feta and Kalamata Olives

Ingredients:

- Cherry tomatoes
- Cucumber, sliced into rounds
- Red onion, cut into small chunks

- Feta cheese, cut into cubes
- Kalamata olives
- Olive oil
- Lemon juice
- Dried oregano
- Salt and black pepper to taste
- Skewers

Instructions:

1. Thread the cherry tomatoes, cucumber slices, red onion chunks, feta cheese cubes, and kalamata olives onto skewers in any order you like.
2. In a small bowl, whisk together olive oil, lemon juice, dried oregano, salt, and black pepper to make a dressing.

3. Brush the skewers with the dressing on all sides.

4. Preheat a grill or grill pan over medium-high heat.

5. Grill the skewers for 2-3 minutes on each side, until the vegetables are slightly charred and the cheese is softened.

6. Remove the skewers from the grill and transfer them to a serving platter.

7. Drizzle any remaining dressing over the skewers.

8. Serve the Greek salad skewers immediately as an appetizer or side dish.

Turkish Spinach and Feta Borek Recipe

Ingredients:

- 1 package of phyllo dough
- 1 lb fresh spinach, washed and chopped
- 1 cup crumbled feta cheese
- 2 cloves garlic, minced
- 1/2 teaspoon salt
- 1/2 teaspoon black pepper
- 1/2 cup olive oil

Instructions:

1. Preheat your oven to 350°F (180°C).

2. In a large mixing bowl, combine the chopped spinach, crumbled feta cheese, minced garlic, salt, and black pepper.

3. Lay a sheet of phyllo dough on a flat surface, and brush it with olive oil. Place another sheet of phyllo dough on top, and brush it with olive oil again. Repeat this process until you have 6 layers of phyllo dough.
4. Cut the phyllo dough into strips that are about 3 inches wide.
5. Take a spoonful of the spinach and feta mixture and place it at the bottom of each strip of phyllo dough. Roll the dough up, tucking in the sides as you go. Repeat this process until all the spinach and feta mixture is used up.
6. Brush the top of the borek with olive oil, and place them on a

baking sheet lined with parchment paper.

7. Bake the borek in the preheated oven for 20-25 minutes, or until they are golden brown.

8. Remove the borek from the oven and allow them to cool for a few minutes before serving.

Baked Feta with Tomatoes and Olives Recipe

Ingredients:

- 1 block of feta cheese
- 2 cups cherry tomatoes
- 1/2 cup Kalamata olives
- 1/4 cup olive oil
- 2 cloves garlic, minced
- 1/4 teaspoon dried oregano

- Salt and pepper, to taste
- Fresh parsley, chopped (optional)

Instructions:

1. Preheat your oven to 400°F (200°C).
2. Place the block of feta cheese in a small baking dish.
3. Arrange the cherry tomatoes and Kalamata olives around the feta cheese.
4. In a small bowl, whisk together the olive oil, minced garlic, dried oregano, salt, and pepper.
5. Pour the olive oil mixture over the feta cheese, cherry tomatoes, and Kalamata olives.
6. Bake the dish in the preheated oven for 15-20 minutes, or until

the feta cheese is soft and slightly golden.

7. Remove the dish from the oven and sprinkle fresh parsley over the top (optional).

8. Serve the baked feta with toasted bread or pita chips.

Muhammara (Roasted Red Pepper and Walnut Dip) Recipe

Ingredients:

- 2 large red bell peppers
- 1 cup walnuts
- 1/2 cup breadcrumbs
- 2 tablespoons lemon juice
- 2 cloves garlic, minced
- 1 teaspoon cumin
- 1/2 teaspoon smoked paprika

- 1/2 teaspoon red pepper flakes
- 1/4 cup olive oil
- Salt and pepper, to taste

Instructions:

1. Preheat your oven to 400°F (200°C).
2. Place the red bell peppers on a baking sheet and roast them in the preheated oven for 20-25 minutes, or until they are soft and slightly charred.
3. Remove the bell peppers from the oven and allow them to cool for a few minutes. Then remove the stems, seeds, and skins.

In a food processor, combine the roasted red bell peppers with the Muhammara recipe:

1. Add the walnuts, breadcrumbs, lemon juice, minced garlic, cumin, smoked paprika, red pepper flakes, olive oil, salt, and pepper to the food processor.

2. Pulse the mixture until it is smooth and well combined.

3. Taste the dip and adjust the seasoning as needed.

4. Transfer the dip to a serving bowl and garnish with chopped walnuts, a drizzle of olive oil, and a sprinkle of smoked paprika.

5. Serve the Muhammara dip with pita chips, fresh vegetables, or crackers.

Stuffed Mushrooms with Feta and Spinach

Ingredients:

- 8 large mushrooms
- 1/2 cup crumbled feta cheese
- 1/2 cup frozen spinach, thawed and drained
- 2 cloves garlic, minced
- 2 tablespoons chopped fresh parsley
- 1/4 teaspoon salt
- 1/4 teaspoon black pepper
- 2 tablespoons olive oil

Instructions:

1. Preheat your oven to 375°F (190°C). Wash and dry the

mushrooms, then remove the stems and set them aside.

2. In a mixing bowl, combine the crumbled feta, thawed spinach, minced garlic, chopped parsley, salt, and black pepper.

3. Use a spoon to fill each mushroom cap with the feta and spinach mixture. Place the filled mushrooms on a baking sheet.

4. Drizzle the olive oil over the stuffed mushrooms and place them in the oven.

5. Bake for 20-25 minutes, or until the mushrooms are tender and the filling is hot and bubbly.

6. Remove the mushrooms from the oven and let them cool for a few minutes before serving.

Tabouli Salad with Parsley and Lemon

Ingredients:

- 1 cup bulgur wheat
- 2 cups boiling water
- 1 large cucumber, seeded and diced
- 2 large tomatoes, diced
- 1 bunch parsley, finely chopped
- 1/4 cup fresh mint leaves, finely chopped
- 1/2 cup lemon juice
- 1/4 cup olive oil
- 2 cloves garlic, minced
- Salt and pepper, to taste

Instructions:

1. Place the bulgur wheat in a large bowl and pour the boiling water over it. Cover the bowl and let it sit for 30 minutes, or until the water is absorbed and the bulgur is tender.

2. Add the diced cucumber, diced tomato, chopped parsley, and chopped mint leaves to the bowl with the bulgur. Mix everything together.

3. In a separate bowl, whisk together the lemon juice, olive oil, minced garlic, salt, and pepper.

4. Pour the dressing over the tabouli salad and toss everything together until the salad is evenly coated with the dressing.

5. Taste the salad and adjust the seasoning as needed. Serve immediately, or cover and refrigerate until ready to serve.

Chickpea and Olive Crostini

Ingredients:

- 1 baguette, sliced into thin rounds
- 1 can chickpeas, drained and rinsed
- 1/2 cup pitted and chopped kalamata olives
- 2 cloves garlic, minced
- 1/4 cup chopped fresh parsley
- 1/4 cup olive oil
- Salt and pepper, to taste

Instructions:

1. Preheat your oven to 375°F (190°C). Arrange the baguette slices on a baking sheet and brush them lightly with olive oil.
2. In a mixing bowl, combine the drained chickpeas, chopped olives, minced garlic, chopped parsley, olive oil, salt, and pepper. Mix everything together.
3. Spoon the chickpea and olive mixture onto each baguette slice.
4. Place the baking sheet in the oven and bake for 10-15 minutes, or until the crostini are crispy and lightly browned.
5. Remove the crostini from the oven and let them cool for a few minutes before serving.

Grilled Halloumi with Honey and Pistachios

Ingredients:

- 8 oz. halloumi cheese, sliced into 1/2-inch thick pieces
- 2 tablespoons olive oil
- 2 tablespoons honey
- 1/4 cup shelled pistachios, chopped
- Fresh mint leaves, for garnish

Instructions:

1. Preheat your grill or grill pan to medium-high heat.
2. Brush the halloumi slices on both sides with olive oil.
3. Grill the halloumi slices for 2-3 minutes on each side, or until they

are lightly charred and heated through.

4. Remove the grilled halloumi from the grill and place it on a serving platter.

5. Drizzle the honey over the top of the halloumi slices.

6. Sprinkle the chopped pistachios over the honey-drizzled halloumi.

7. Garnish with fresh mint leaves.

8. Serve immediately while the halloumi is still warm.

Tomato and Mozzarella Bruschetta with Balsamic Glaze

Ingredients:

- 1 large tomato, diced
- 1/2 cup fresh mozzarella, diced

- 1/4 cup fresh basil, chopped
- 1 garlic clove, minced
- 1 tablespoon olive oil
- Salt and pepper, to taste
- 8 slices of French bread, sliced diagonally
- Balsamic glaze for drizzling

Directions:

1. Preheat oven to 400°F.
2. In a small bowl, mix together the diced tomato, mozzarella, basil, garlic, olive oil, salt and pepper.
3. Place the sliced bread on a baking sheet and brush each slice with olive oil.
4. Top each slice with the tomato and mozzarella mixture.

5. Bake for 8-10 minutes or until bread is toasted and cheese is melted.
6. Remove from oven and drizzle with balsamic glaze.
7. Serve immediately.

Roasted Beet and Goat Cheese Crostini

Ingredients:

- 3 medium beets, peeled and sliced
- 1 tablespoon olive oil
- Salt and pepper, to taste
- 8 slices of French bread, sliced diagonally
- 4 ounces of goat cheese, softened
- 1/4 cup chopped walnuts

Directions:

1. Preheat oven to 375°F.
2. In a large bowl, toss the sliced beets with olive oil, salt, and pepper.
3. Spread the beets in a single layer on a baking sheet and roast for 20-25 minutes, or until tender.
4. Meanwhile, toast the slices of bread on a separate baking sheet in the oven for 5-7 minutes, or until lightly golden brown.
5. Spread each slice of bread with a generous amount of goat cheese.
6. Top each slice with a few roasted beet slices and sprinkle with chopped walnuts.
7. Serve immediately.

Section 2: Soups and Salads

Greek Lentil Soup with Feta Cheese

Ingredients:

- 1 cup brown or green lentils, rinsed and drained
- 1 onion, chopped
- 3 cloves garlic, minced
- 1 carrot, chopped
- 1 celery stalk, chopped
- 1 bay leaf
- 4 cups vegetable broth
- 1 can diced tomatoes
- 1 tbsp tomato paste
- 1 tbsp dried oregano
- 1/4 tsp salt
- 1/4 tsp black pepper

- 1/2 cup crumbled feta cheese
- Fresh parsley, chopped (optional)

Directions:

1. In a large pot or Dutch oven, heat 1 tablespoon of olive oil over medium heat.
2. Add onion, garlic, carrot, and celery, and sauté until softened, about 5 minutes.
3. Add the lentils, bay leaf, vegetable broth, diced tomatoes, tomato paste, oregano, salt, and pepper. Stir well to combine.
4. Bring the soup to a boil, then reduce heat and simmer for 25-30 minutes or until lentils are tender.
5. Remove the bay leaf and use an immersion blender to puree the

soup until smooth (alternatively, transfer soup to a blender and puree in batches).

6. Serve hot, topped with crumbled feta cheese and fresh parsley, if desired.

Moroccan Carrot Salad with Cumin Dressing

Ingredients:

- 4-5 medium carrots, peeled and grated
- 1/4 cup chopped fresh parsley
- 1/4 cup chopped fresh cilantro
- 1/4 cup chopped green onion
- 1/4 cup chopped dried apricots
- 1/4 cup sliced almonds, toasted
- 2 tbsp olive oil

- 1 tbsp fresh lemon juice
- 1 tsp honey
- 1 tsp ground cumin
- 1/4 tsp salt
- 1/4 tsp black pepper

Directions:

1. In a large bowl, combine grated carrots, parsley, cilantro, green onion, dried apricots, and sliced almonds.

2. In a small bowl, whisk together olive oil, lemon juice, honey, cumin, salt, and black pepper.

3. Pour the dressing over the salad and toss well to combine.

4. Serve at room temperature or chilled.

Tuscan Bean and Tomato Soup

Ingredients:

- 1 tbsp olive oil
- 1 onion, chopped
- 3 cloves garlic, minced
- 1 can diced tomatoes
- 2 cans white beans, rinsed and drained
- 4 cups vegetable broth
- 1 tsp dried thyme
- 1 tsp dried rosemary
- 1/4 tsp red pepper flakes
- Salt and black pepper to taste
- Fresh parsley, chopped (optional)

Directions:

1. In a large pot or Dutch oven, heat olive oil over medium heat.

2. Add onion and garlic, and sauté until softened, about 5 minutes.

3. Add diced tomatoes, white beans, vegetable broth, thyme, rosemary, red pepper flakes, salt, and black pepper. Stir well to combine.

4. Bring the soup to a boil, then reduce heat and simmer for 15-20 minutes or until the flavors are well combined and the soup is heated through.

5. Serve hot, topped with fresh parsley, if desired.

Lebanese Fattoush Salad with Pita Chips

Ingredients:

- 1 head of romaine lettuce, chopped

- 1 medium cucumber, diced
- 3 medium tomatoes, diced
- 1 small red onion, thinly sliced
- 1/2 cup chopped fresh parsley
- 1/2 cup chopped fresh mint
- 1/4 cup chopped fresh cilantro
- 1/4 cup extra virgin olive oil
- 1/4 cup fresh lemon juice
- 2 cloves garlic, minced
- 1 teaspoon sumac
- Salt and pepper, to taste
- 4 whole wheat pita bread, cut into small pieces and toasted

Instructions:

1. In a large bowl, combine the chopped lettuce, cucumber, tomatoes, and red onion.

2. In a separate bowl, whisk together the olive oil, lemon juice, garlic, sumac, salt, and pepper to make the dressing.
3. Pour the dressing over the salad and toss to coat.
4. Add the chopped herbs to the salad and toss again.
5. Add the toasted pita pieces to the salad just before serving, to prevent them from getting soggy.

Italian Panzanella Salad with Fresh Basil and Balsamic Vinaigrette

Ingredients:

- 1 large loaf of stale Italian bread, cut into bite-sized pieces
- 1 medium cucumber, diced

- 3 medium tomatoes, diced
- 1 small red onion, thinly sliced
- 1/2 cup chopped fresh basil
- 1/4 cup extra virgin olive oil
- 1/4 cup balsamic vinegar
- Salt and pepper, to taste

Instructions:

1. In a large bowl, combine the bread, cucumber, tomatoes, and red onion.
2. In a separate bowl, whisk together the olive oil, balsamic vinegar, salt, and pepper to make the dressing.
3. Pour the dressing over the salad and toss to coat.
4. Add the chopped basil to the salad and toss again.

5. Let the salad sit for at least 30 minutes before serving, to allow the bread to soak up the dressing and become tender.

Turkish Red Lentil Soup with Mint and Lemon

Ingredients:

- 1 cup red lentils, rinsed and drained
- 1 medium onion, chopped
- 2 cloves garlic, minced
- 2 medium carrots, peeled and chopped
- 2 tablespoons tomato paste
- 1 teaspoon ground cumin
- 1/2 teaspoon paprika
- 4 cups vegetable broth

- Juice of 1 lemon
- Salt and pepper, to taste
- 1/4 cup chopped fresh mint

Instructions:

1. In a large pot, sauté the onion and garlic in a little bit of olive oil until they are softened.
2. Add the chopped carrots, tomato paste, cumin, and paprika to the pot, and stir well.
3. Add the lentils and vegetable broth to the pot, and bring to a boil.
4. Reduce the heat and let the soup simmer for about 20 minutes, or until the lentils are tender.
5. Use an immersion blender or transfer the soup to a blender and puree until smooth.

6. Add the lemon juice, salt, and pepper to the soup, and stir well.
7. Serve the soup hot, garnished with chopped fresh mint.

Spanish Gazpacho with Croutons and Olive Oil

Ingredients:

- 6 medium ripe tomatoes, cored and roughly chopped
- 1 medium cucumber, peeled and roughly chopped
- 1 medium red bell pepper, seeded and roughly chopped
- 2 cloves garlic, minced
- 1/4 cup extra virgin olive oil
- 2 tablespoons sherry vinegar
- Salt and pepper, to taste

- Croutons and additional olive oil, for serving

Instructions:

1. In a blender or food processor, combine the chopped tomatoes, cucumber, red bell pepper, and garlic.
2. Blend until the mixture is smooth and well-combined.
3. With the blender still running, slowly pour in the olive oil and sherry vinegar, and continue blending until the mixture is emulsified.
4. Season the gazpacho with salt and pepper, to taste.

5. Chill the gazpacho in the refrigerator for at least 1 hour, to allow the flavors to meld together.
6. Serve the gazpacho cold, garnished with croutons and a drizzle of olive oil.

Israeli Quinoa Tabbouleh Salad with Parsley and Lemon

Ingredients:
- 1 cup quinoa
- 2 cups water
- 1/4 cup extra-virgin olive oil
- 1/4 cup freshly squeezed lemon juice
- 2 cloves garlic, minced
- 1/2 teaspoon salt
- 1/4 teaspoon black pepper

- 2 cups chopped fresh parsley leaves
- 1/2 cup chopped fresh mint leaves
- 1 large tomato, chopped
- 1/2 cucumber, chopped
- 1/2 red onion, chopped

Instructions:

1. Rinse the quinoa in a fine mesh strainer under cold running water.
2. In a medium saucepan, bring the quinoa and water to a boil. Reduce heat to low and simmer, covered, for 15-20 minutes or until the water is absorbed and the quinoa is tender.
3.

4. In a small bowl, whisk together the olive oil, lemon juice, garlic, salt, and pepper.

5. In a large bowl, combine the cooked quinoa, parsley, mint, tomato, cucumber, and red onion.

6. Pour the dressing over the salad and toss to coat. Serve chilled or at room temperature.

Greek Avgolemono Soup with Orzo and Spinach

Ingredients:
- 8 cups vegetable broth
- 1 cup uncooked orzo pasta
- 4 eggs
- 1/2 cup freshly squeezed lemon juice

- 2 cups fresh spinach leaves
- Salt and black pepper, to taste

Instructions:

1. In a large pot, bring the vegetable broth to a boil. Add the orzo and cook for 8-10 minutes or until tender.
2. In a medium bowl, whisk together the eggs and lemon juice until frothy.
3. Gradually add a ladleful of the hot broth to the egg mixture, whisking constantly.
4. Slowly pour the egg mixture back into the pot of soup, whisking constantly.

5. Add the spinach to the pot and cook for 2-3 minutes or until wilted.
6. Season the soup with salt and black pepper to taste. Serve hot.

Moroccan Chickpea Salad with Harissa Dressing

Ingredients:

- 2 cans chickpeas, drained and rinsed
- 1/2 cup chopped fresh parsley leaves
- 1/2 cup chopped fresh cilantro leaves
- 1/2 cup chopped red onion
- 1/2 cup chopped roasted red pepper

- 1/2 cup chopped cucumber
- 1/4 cup freshly squeezed lemon juice
- 1/4 cup extra-virgin olive oil
- 2 teaspoons harissa paste
- Salt and black pepper, to taste

Instructions:

1. In a large bowl, combine the chickpeas, parsley, cilantro, red onion, roasted red pepper, and cucumber.
2. In a small bowl, whisk together the lemon juice, olive oil, harissa paste, salt, and black pepper.
3. Pour the dressing over the salad and toss to coat. Serve chilled or at room temperature.

Italian Minestrone Soup with Pesto and Parmesan Cheese

Ingredients:

- 2 tablespoons olive oil
- 1 onion, chopped
- 2 cloves garlic, minced
- 2 carrots, chopped
- 2 celery stalks, chopped
- 1 zucchini, chopped
- 1 yellow squash, chopped
- 1 can diced tomatoes
- 6 cups vegetable broth
- 1 cup small pasta, such as ditalini or small shells
- 1/4 cup pesto sauce
- 1/4 cup grated Parmesan

Instructions:

1. In a large pot, heat the olive oil over medium heat. Add the onion and garlic and cook until softened, about 5 minutes.
2. Add the carrots, celery, zucchini, and yellow squash and cook for 5-7 minutes, or until the vegetables are tender.
3. Add the diced tomatoes (with their juice) and vegetable broth to the pot. Bring to a boil, then reduce the heat and simmer for 10-15 minutes.
4. Add the pasta to the pot and cook for an additional 10-12 minutes, or until the pasta is tender.
5. Stir in the pesto sauce and grated Parmesan cheese.

6. Serve hot, garnished with additional grated Parmesan cheese and a drizzle of olive oil, if desired.

Note: You can use any type of pasta you prefer in this recipe. Just adjust the cooking time accordingly. Also, feel free to add any other vegetables you have on hand, such as bell peppers, green beans, or kale.

Lebanese Tabbouleh Salad with Bulgur Wheat and Cucumber

Ingredients:
- 1 cup bulgur wheat
- 1 large cucumber, diced
- 1 cup chopped fresh parsley

- 1/2 cup chopped fresh mint
- 3 medium tomatoes, diced
- 1/2 red onion, finely chopped
- Juice of 2 lemons
- 1/4 cup extra-virgin olive oil
- Salt and pepper to taste

Directions:

1. Rinse the bulgur wheat in a fine mesh strainer and place in a large mixing bowl.
2. Pour boiling water over the bulgur wheat and let it soak for 30 minutes.
3. Drain any excess water from the bulgur wheat and add cucumber, parsley, mint, tomatoes, and red onion.

4. In a small mixing bowl, whisk together the lemon juice, olive oil, salt, and pepper.

5. Pour the dressing over the salad and mix well.

6. Serve chilled or at room temperature.

Spanish White Bean and Chorizo Soup with Paprika and Garlic

Ingredients:

- 2 tablespoons olive oil
- 1 medium onion, finely chopped
- 3 cloves garlic, minced
- 1/2 teaspoon smoked paprika
- 1 can of white beans, drained and rinsed
- 4 cups vegetable broth

- 1/2 pound chorizo sausage, sliced
- Salt and pepper to taste

Directions:

1. Heat the olive oil in a large soup pot over medium heat.
2. Add the onion and garlic and sauté until soft and translucent.
3. Add the smoked paprika and stir well.
4. Add the white beans and vegetable broth and bring to a boil.
5. Reduce the heat to low and simmer for 15 minutes.
6. In a separate pan, fry the sliced chorizo until crispy.
7. Add the chorizo to the soup and stir well.
8. Serve hot with crusty bread.

Turkish Cacik Salad with Yogurt, Cucumber and Mint

Ingredients:

- 2 cups plain Greek yogurt
- 1 large cucumber, grated
- 1/4 cup chopped fresh mint
- 1 clove garlic, minced
- 2 tablespoons extra-virgin olive oil
- Salt and pepper to taste

Directions:

1. In a large mixing bowl, combine the Greek yogurt, grated cucumber, chopped mint, and minced garlic.
2. Add the olive oil and mix well.

3. Season with salt and pepper to taste.

4. Chill in the refrigerator for at least 30 minutes before serving.

5. Serve as a side dish or dip with pita bread.

Greek Tomato and Feta Salad with Red Onion and Olives

Ingredients:

- 4 large tomatoes, diced
- 1/2 red onion, thinly sliced
- 1/2 cup crumbled feta cheese
- 1/4 cup pitted Kalamata olives
- 2 tablespoons extra-virgin olive oil
- 1 tablespoon red wine vinegar
- 1/2 teaspoon dried oregano
- Salt and pepper to taste

Directions:

1. In a large mixing bowl, combine the diced tomatoes, thinly sliced red onion, crumbled feta cheese, and pitted Kalamata olives.

2. In a separate mixing bowl, whisk together the olive oil, red wine vinegar, dried oregano, salt, and pepper.

3. Pour the dressing over the salad and mix well.

4. Serve chilled or at room temperature.

5. Garnish with additional feta cheese and olives, if desired.

Moroccan Harira Soup with Chickpeas and Lentils

Ingredients:

- 1 cup red lentils, rinsed and drained
- 1 can chickpeas, rinsed and drained
- 1 onion, finely chopped
- 2 garlic cloves, minced
- 2 teaspoons ground cumin
- 1 teaspoon ground cinnamon
- 1 teaspoon ground ginger
- 1/2 teaspoon turmeric
- 1/4 teaspoon cayenne pepper
- 1/4 teaspoon black pepper
- 1/4 teaspoon salt
- 4 cups vegetable broth
- 1 can diced tomatoes
- 1/4 cup chopped fresh cilantro

- Juice of 1/2 lemon

Instructions:

1. In a large pot, sauté the onion and garlic until the onion is soft and translucent.
2. Add the lentils, chickpeas, cumin, cinnamon, ginger, turmeric, cayenne pepper, black pepper, and salt to the pot. Stir well to coat the lentils and chickpeas in the spices.
3. Add the vegetable broth and diced tomatoes to the pot. Bring the soup to a boil, then reduce the heat and simmer for 30 minutes, or until the lentils are tender.
4. Remove the pot from the heat and stir in the cilantro and lemon juice.

5. Use an immersion blender or transfer the soup to a blender and blend until smooth.

6. Serve hot, garnished with additional cilantro, if desired.

Italian Caprese Salad with Fresh Mozzarella and Basil

Ingredients:

- 3 large tomatoes, sliced
- 8 oz. fresh mozzarella, sliced
- 1/4 cup fresh basil leaves
- 2 tablespoons extra-virgin olive oil
- 1 tablespoon balsamic vinegar
- Salt and pepper to taste

Instructions:

- Arrange the tomato and mozzarella slices on a large platter, alternating between the two.
- Sprinkle the basil leaves over the top of the tomato and mozzarella slices.
- Drizzle the olive oil and balsamic vinegar over the top of the salad.
- Season the salad with salt and pepper to taste.
- Serve immediately.

Lebanese Baba Ghanoush Salad with Roasted Eggplant and Tahini

Ingredients:
2 medium eggplants, halved lengthwise
2 tablespoons tahini

2 garlic cloves, minced

2 tablespoons lemon juice

1/4 teaspoon ground cumin

Salt and pepper to taste

1/4 cup chopped fresh parsley

1/4 cup chopped fresh mint

Instructions:

1. Preheat the oven to 375°F. Line a baking sheet with parchment paper.

2. Place the eggplant halves on the prepared baking sheet, cut side down.

3. Bake the eggplant for 25-30 minutes, or until the skin is charred and the flesh is soft.

4. Remove the eggplant from the oven and let it cool for 10 minutes.

5. Scoop the flesh out of the eggplant skins and transfer it to a food processor.

6. Add the tahini, garlic, lemon juice, cumin, salt, and pepper to the food processor. Pulse until smooth.

7. Transfer the baba ghanoush to a serving bowl and sprinkle the parsley and mint over the top.

8. Serve chilled or at room temperature.

Spanish Potato and Garlic Soup with Smoked Paprika

Ingredients:
- 2 tablespoons olive oil
- 1 onion, chopped
- 4 garlic cloves, minced

- 4 large potatoes, peeled and diced
- 4 cups vegetable broth
- 1 teaspoon smoked paprika
- Salt and pepper to taste
- Chopped fresh parsley for garnish

Instructions:

1. In a large pot, heat the olive oil over medium heat.
2. Add the chopped onion and minced garlic to the pot. Sauté until the onion is translucent and the garlic is fragrant.
3. Add the diced potatoes to the pot and stir to coat them in the oil and onion-garlic mixture.
4. Pour the vegetable broth into the pot and bring the mixture to a boil.

5. Reduce the heat to low and simmer the soup for 20-25 minutes, or until the potatoes are tender.
6. Use an immersion blender or transfer the soup to a blender and blend until smooth.
7. Stir in the smoked paprika and season the soup with salt and pepper to taste.
8. Serve hot, garnished with chopped fresh parsley.

Turkish Shepherd's Salad with Tomato, Cucumber and Parsley

Ingredients:
- 3 large tomatoes, diced
- 2 cucumbers, diced

- 1 small red onion, diced
- 1/4 cup chopped fresh parsley
- 2 tablespoons extra-virgin olive oil
- 1 tablespoon lemon juice
- Salt and pepper to taste

Instructions:

1. In a large bowl, combine the diced tomatoes, cucumbers, and red onion.
2. Add the chopped parsley to the bowl and stir to combine.
3. In a small bowl, whisk together the olive oil and lemon juice. Drizzle the mixture over the salad and toss to coat.
4. Season the salad with salt and pepper to taste.

5. Serve chilled or at room temperature.

Section 3: Main Courses

Stuffed Eggplant with Spiced Lentils and Feta

Ingredients:

- 2 medium-sized eggplants
- 1 cup cooked lentils
- 1/2 cup crumbled feta cheese
- 1/4 cup chopped fresh parsley
- 2 cloves garlic, minced
- 1/2 teaspoon ground cumin
- 1/2 teaspoon ground coriander
- 1/4 teaspoon smoked paprika
- 1/4 teaspoon ground cinnamon
- 1 tablespoon olive oil
- Salt and black pepper, to taste

Instructions:

1. Preheat oven to 375°F (190°C).

2. Cut the eggplants in half lengthwise and scoop out the flesh, leaving a 1/2-inch border around the edges. Reserve the flesh.

3. In a skillet, heat olive oil over medium heat. Add the eggplant flesh, garlic, cumin, coriander, paprika, and cinnamon. Cook for 5-7 minutes or until the eggplant is tender.

4. Add the cooked lentils and parsley to the skillet and stir to combine. Season with salt and pepper to taste.

5. Spoon the lentil mixture into the eggplant halves and sprinkle with crumbled feta cheese.

6. Place the stuffed eggplants on a baking sheet and bake for 30-35 minutes or until the eggplant is tender and the cheese is melted and golden brown.
7. Serve immediately.

Spinach and Feta Pie with Homemade Phyllo

Ingredients:

For the phyllo dough:

- 2 cups all-purpose flour
- 1/4 teaspoon salt
- 2 tablespoons olive oil
- 1/2 cup warm water

For the filling:

- 1 lb spinach, chopped

- 1/2 lb feta cheese, crumbled
- 1 onion, chopped
- 3 tablespoons olive oil
- 1/4 teaspoon ground nutmeg
- Salt and black pepper, to taste

Instructions:

1. In a large bowl, whisk together the flour and salt. Make a well in the center and add the olive oil and warm water. Stir with a wooden spoon until the dough comes together.
2. Turn the dough out onto a lightly floured surface and knead for 5-7 minutes or until smooth and elastic.
3. Divide the dough into 8 equal pieces and roll each piece into a

ball. Cover the dough balls with a damp towel and let rest for 30 minutes.

4. Preheat oven to 375°F (190°C).

5. In a skillet, heat 2 tablespoons of olive oil over medium heat. Add the chopped onion and sauté for 5-7 minutes or until translucent.

6. Add the chopped spinach to the skillet and cook until wilted, about 3-4 minutes.

7. Remove the skillet from the heat and add the crumbled feta cheese, nutmeg, salt, and pepper. Stir to combine.

8. On a lightly floured surface, roll out each dough ball into a thin circle.

9. Grease a 9-inch pie dish with olive oil and lay one circle of dough on the bottom. Brush with olive oil and add another circle of dough on top, repeating the process until you have 4 layers of dough.

10. Spoon the spinach and feta mixture onto the phyllo layers in the pie dish.

11. Cover the filling with the remaining 4 circles of dough, brushing each layer with olive oil.

12. Bake for 35-40 minutes or until the phyllo is golden brown and crisp.

13. Let the pie cool for 10 minutes before slicing and serving.

Chickpea and Vegetable Tagine with Couscous

Ingredients:

- 1 1/2 cups couscous
- 2 cups water or vegetable broth
- 1/4 teaspoon salt
- 1 tablespoon olive oil
- Optional add-ins: chopped fresh herbs, toasted nuts, dried fruits, sautéed vegetables

Instructions:

1. In a saucepan, bring the water or vegetable broth to a boil.
2. Add the salt and olive oil to the water.
3. Stir in the couscous and remove from heat.

4. Cover the saucepan with a lid and let sit for 5-10 minutes or until the liquid is absorbed.

5. Use a fork to fluff the couscous and break up any clumps.

6. Add any optional add-ins and stir to combine.

7. Serve immediately as a side dish or use as a base for the Chickpea and Vegetable Tagine.

Mushroom Risotto with Roasted Garlic and Parmesan

Ingredients:

- 1 cup arborio rice
- 1 quart vegetable or chicken broth
- 2 tablespoons olive oil
- 1 large onion, diced

- 1 pound mushrooms, sliced
- 4 cloves roasted garlic, minced
- 1/2 cup grated Parmesan cheese
- Salt and pepper, to taste
- Fresh parsley, chopped (optional)

Instructions:

1. In a large saucepan, bring the broth to a simmer and keep it hot on low heat.

2. In another large saucepan, heat the olive oil over medium-high heat. Add the onion and cook for 3-4 minutes, until softened.

3. Add the mushrooms to the onion and cook until they are tender and browned, about 5-7 minutes.

4. Add the rice to the mushroom mixture and stir to coat it with the oil.

5. Begin adding the hot broth, one ladleful at a time, stirring constantly and waiting for the liquid to be absorbed before adding more. Keep stirring and adding broth until the rice is tender and creamy, about 20-25 minutes.

6. Stir in the roasted garlic and Parmesan cheese, and season with salt and pepper to taste.

7. Serve the risotto hot, garnished with chopped parsley if desired.

Mediterranean Vegetable Stew with Cannellini Beans

Ingredients:

- 2 tablespoons olive oil
- 1 large onion, diced
- 3 cloves garlic, minced
- 2 bell peppers, diced
- 1 eggplant, diced
- 1 zucchini, diced
- 1 can diced tomatoes
- 1 can cannellini beans, drained and rinsed
- 1 teaspoon dried oregano
- Salt and pepper, to taste
- Fresh parsley, chopped (optional)

Instructions:

1. Heat the olive oil in a large saucepan or Dutch oven over

medium-high heat. Add the onion and garlic and cook for 3-4 minutes, until softened.

2. Add the bell peppers, eggplant, and zucchini to the pan and cook for 5-7 minutes, until they begin to soften.

3. Add the diced tomatoes (including their juice), cannellini beans, oregano, and a pinch of salt and pepper. Bring to a simmer and cook for 15-20 minutes, until the vegetables are tender and the stew has thickened slightly.

4. Serve the stew hot, garnished with chopped parsley if desired.

Falafel with Tahini Sauce
Pita Bread

Ingredients:

- 1 can chickpeas, drained and rinsed
- 1/2 cup chopped fresh parsley
- 1/2 cup chopped fresh cilantro
- 1/2 onion, chopped
- 2 cloves garlic, minced
- 1 teaspoon ground cumin
- 1/2 teaspoon ground coriander
- Salt and pepper, to taste
- 1/4 cup all-purpose flour
- 1/4 teaspoon baking powder
- 1/4 cup vegetable oil
- Tahini sauce, for serving
- Pita bread, for serving

Instructions:

1. In a food processor, pulse together the chickpeas, parsley, cilantro, onion, garlic, cumin, coriander, salt, and pepper until well combined but still slightly chunky.
2. Add the flour and baking powder and pulse again until the mixture comes together in a dough.
3. Heat the vegetable oil in a large skillet over medium heat.
4. Use a small cookie scoop or spoon to form the falafel mixture into small balls and flatten them slightly.
5. Fry the falafel in the hot oil for 3-4 minutes per side, until golden brown and crispy. You may need to do this in batches, depending on the size of your skillet.

6. Serve the hot falafel with tahini sauce and pita bread on the side.

Caprese Salad with Grilled Portobello Mushrooms

Ingredients:

- 4 large portobello mushrooms, stems removed
- 2 tablespoons olive oil
- Salt and pepper, to taste
- 4 large ripe tomatoes, sliced
- 1 pound fresh mozzarella, sliced
- 1/4 cup fresh basil leaves, torn
- Balsamic glaze, for serving

Instructions:

1. Preheat a grill or grill pan to medium-high heat.

2. Brush the portobello mushrooms with olive oil and season with salt and pepper.
3. Grill the mushrooms for 3-4 minutes per side, until tender and lightly charred.
4. Arrange the sliced tomatoes, mozzarella, and grilled portobello mushrooms on a large platter.
5. Drizzle the caprese salad with balsamic glaze and sprinkle with fresh torn basil leaves.
6. Serve the salad immediately, while the mushrooms are still warm.

Roasted Eggplant and Tomato Pasta with Basil and Pine Nuts

Ingredients:

- 1 medium eggplant, chopped into small cubes
- 2 cups cherry tomatoes
- 4 cloves garlic, minced
- 1/4 cup pine nuts
- 1/2 cup fresh basil leaves, chopped
- 1/4 cup olive oil
- Salt and pepper to taste
- 1 pound pasta of your choice (spaghetti, penne, fusilli)

Instructions:

1. Preheat the oven to 400°F (200°C).

2. Place the eggplant cubes and cherry tomatoes in a large baking dish.

3. In a small bowl, whisk together the minced garlic, olive oil, salt, and pepper.

4. Drizzle the garlic mixture over the eggplant and tomatoes, and toss everything together to ensure that the vegetables are coated evenly.

5. Roast the vegetables in the oven for 25-30 minutes, or until they are soft and slightly caramelized.

6. While the vegetables are roasting, cook the pasta according to package instructions.

7. In a small frying pan, toast the pine nuts over medium heat until they are golden brown.

8. Once the pasta is cooked, drain it and return it to the pot.

9. Add the roasted eggplant and tomato mixture to the pot, along with the chopped basil leaves and toasted pine nuts.

10. Toss everything together until the pasta is coated evenly with the vegetable mixture.

11. Serve the pasta hot, garnished with additional basil leaves and a sprinkle of parmesan cheese, if desired.

Spanakopita (Greek Spinach Pie) with Feta and Phyllo Pastry

Ingredients:

- 10 oz. frozen spinach, thawed and drained
- 1/2 cup crumbled feta cheese
- 1/4 cup grated parmesan cheese
- 1/4 cup chopped fresh dill
- 1/4 cup chopped fresh parsley
- 1/4 cup chopped green onions
- 1/4 cup olive oil
- Salt and pepper to taste
- 8-10 sheets phyllo pastry, thawed
- 1/4 cup melted butter

Instructions:

1. Preheat the oven to 375°F (190°C).
2. In a large bowl, combine the thawed spinach, crumbled feta cheese, grated parmesan cheese, chopped dill, chopped parsley, chopped green onions, olive oil,

salt, and pepper. Mix everything together until well combined.

3. On a clean surface, lay out one sheet of phyllo pastry and brush it lightly with melted butter. Place another sheet of phyllo on top of the first sheet and brush it with butter as well. Repeat with the remaining phyllo sheets, brushing each sheet with butter as you go.

4. Spoon the spinach and feta mixture onto the phyllo pastry, leaving about 1 inch of space around the edges.

5. Fold the edges of the phyllo pastry over the spinach mixture to form a rectangle.

6. Brush the top of the pastry with melted butter.

7. Bake the spanakopita in the preheated oven for 25-30 minutes, or until the pastry is golden brown and crispy.
8. Let the spanakopita cool for a few minutes before slicing it into pieces and serving.

Lebanese Mujadara (Lentils and Rice) with Caramelized Onions

Ingredients:
- 1 cup brown lentils
- 1/2 cup white rice
- 2 cups water
- 1/4 cup olive oil
- 3 large onions, sliced thinly
- Salt and pepper to taste

Instructions:

1. Rinse the lentils and rice with cold water and set aside.

2. In a large pot, bring 2 cups of water to a boil over high heat. Add the lentils and rice to the pot and stir to combine.

3. Reduce the heat to low and cover the pot. Simmer the lentils and rice for 20-25 minutes, or until they are tender and the water has been absorbed.

4. While the lentils and rice are cooking, heat the olive oil in a large skillet over medium heat. Add the sliced onions to the skillet and stir to coat them with the oil.

5. Cook the onions, stirring occasionally, for 15-20 minutes, or

until they are soft and caramelized. Season with salt and pepper to taste.

6. Once the lentils and rice are cooked, remove the pot from the heat and let it sit for 5-10 minutes.

7. Fluff the lentils and rice with a fork, then transfer them to a large serving bowl.

8. Top the lentils and rice with the caramelized onions, using a slotted spoon to leave behind any excess oil.

9. Serve the mujadara hot or at room temperature, garnished with fresh parsley or cilantro if desired.

Note: You can also add spices like cumin or coriander to the lentils and rice while they are cooking to add extra flavor to the dish.

Israeli Shakshuka (Eggs Poached in Spicy Tomato Sauce)

Ingredients:

- 2 tbsp olive oil
- 1 onion, chopped
- 3 garlic cloves, minced
- 1 red bell pepper, chopped
- 1 tsp ground cumin
- 1 tsp smoked paprika
- 1/4 tsp cayenne pepper
- 1 can (28 oz) crushed tomatoes
- 4-6 eggs
- Salt and pepper to taste
- Fresh parsley, chopped (optional)

Instructions:

1. Heat the olive oil in a large skillet over medium-high heat.
2. Add the onion and garlic and sauté for 2-3 minutes until softened.
3. Add the red bell pepper and spices and continue to sauté for another 2-3 minutes until the pepper has softened.
4. Add the crushed tomatoes and bring to a simmer.
5. Crack the eggs into the tomato sauce, making sure to space them out evenly.
6. Cover the skillet and simmer for 5-10 minutes until the egg whites are set but the yolks are still runny.

7. Sprinkle with salt, pepper, and fresh parsley (if using) and serve with crusty bread.

Moroccan Harira Soup with Chickpeas and Lentils

Ingredients:

- 2 tbsp olive oil
- 1 onion, chopped
- 3 garlic cloves, minced
- 1 carrot, chopped
- 1 celery stalk, chopped
- 1 tsp ground cumin
- 1 tsp ground coriander
- 1/2 tsp ground ginger
- 1/4 tsp cinnamon
- 1 can (14 oz) diced tomatoes
- 4 cups vegetable broth

- 1 can (15 oz) chickpeas, drained and rinsed
- 1/2 cup red lentils, rinsed
- Salt and pepper to taste
- Fresh cilantro, chopped (optional)

Instructions:

1. Heat the olive oil in a large pot over medium-high heat.
2. Add the onion and garlic and sauté for 2-3 minutes until softened.
3. Add the carrot and celery and continue to sauté for another 2-3 minutes until the vegetables have softened.
4. Add the spices and sauté for another minute until fragrant.
5. Add the diced tomatoes, vegetable broth, chickpeas, and lentils.

6. Bring to a boil, then reduce heat and simmer for 20-25 minutes until the lentils are cooked through.
7. Season with salt and pepper to taste, and sprinkle with fresh cilantro (if using) before serving.

Greek Gigantes Plaki (Giant Beans in Tomato Sauce) with Feta and Olives

Ingredients:

- 2 cans (15 oz each) giant white beans, drained and rinsed
- 1 onion, chopped
- 3 garlic cloves, minced
- 1 red bell pepper, chopped
- 1 can (14 oz) diced tomatoes

- 1/2 cup vegetable broth
- 1 tbsp tomato paste
- 1 tsp dried oregano
- Salt and pepper to taste
- Feta cheese, crumbled
- Kalamata olives, pitted and chopped
- Fresh parsley, chopped (optional)

Instructions:

1. Preheat the oven to 375°F.
2. In a large oven-safe skillet, heat some olive oil over medium-high heat.
3. Add the chopped onion and sauté for 2-3 minutes until softened.
4. Add the garlic and red bell pepper and sauté for another 2-3 minutes until softened.

5. Add the diced tomatoes, vegetable broth, tomato paste, oregano, salt, and pepper. Stir well.
6. Add the drained and rinsed beans to the skillet and stir to coat them in the tomato sauce.
7. Bake in the preheated oven for 20-25 minutes until the beans are tender and the sauce has thickened.
8. Sprinkle with crumbled feta cheese, chopped kalamata olives, and fresh parsley (if using) before serving.

Tuscan White Bean Soup with Rosemary and Parmesan

Ingredients:

- 2 tbsp olive oil
- 1 onion, chopped
- 3 garlic cloves, minced
- 1 carrot, chopped
- 1 celery stalk, chopped
- 1 tsp dried rosemary
- 1 can (14 oz) diced tomatoes
- 4 cups vegetable broth
- 2 cans (15 oz each) cannellini beans, drained and rinsed
- Salt and pepper to taste
- Parmesan cheese, grated
- Fresh parsley, chopped (optional)

Instructions:

1. Heat the olive oil in a large pot over medium-high heat.
2. Add the onion and garlic and sauté for 2-3 minutes until softened.

3. Add the carrot and celery and continue to sauté for another 2-3 minutes until the vegetables have softened.
4. Add the dried rosemary and sauté for another minute until fragrant.
5. Add the diced tomatoes, vegetable broth, and cannellini beans.
6. Bring to a boil, then reduce heat and simmer for 20-25 minutes until the soup has thickened and the vegetables are tender.
7. Season with salt and pepper to taste.
8. Serve with grated Parmesan cheese and fresh parsley (if using).

Lebanese Fattoush Salad with Grilled Halloumi Cheese

Ingredients:

- 1 head romaine lettuce, chopped
- 1 cucumber, chopped
- 1 tomato, chopped
- 1 green bell pepper, chopped
- 1 red onion, thinly sliced
- 1/4 cup chopped fresh parsley
- 1/4 cup chopped fresh mint
- 1/4 cup chopped fresh cilantro
- 1/4 cup lemon juice
- 1/4 cup olive oil
- 1 garlic clove, minced
- Salt and pepper to taste
- 8 oz halloumi cheese, sliced
- Pita bread, toasted and chopped

Instructions:

1. In a large bowl, combine the chopped lettuce, cucumber, tomato, bell pepper, red onion, parsley, mint, and cilantro.
2. In a small bowl, whisk together the lemon juice, olive oil, garlic, salt, and pepper to make the dressing.
3. Pour the dressing over the salad and toss to coat.
4. Heat a grill or grill pan over high heat.
5. Grill the halloumi cheese slices for 2-3 minutes per side until browned and slightly crispy.
6. Add the chopped pita bread to the salad and toss to combine.
7. Serve the salad with the grilled halloumi cheese on top.

Spanish Paella with Artichokes and Peas

Ingredients:

- 1 onion, chopped
- 2 cloves garlic, minced
- 2 cups Arborio rice
- 4 cups vegetable broth
- 1/2 tsp smoked paprika
- 1/4 tsp saffron threads
- 1 can artichoke hearts, drained and quartered
- 1 cup frozen peas
- 1 red bell pepper, sliced
- 1 tbsp olive oil
- Salt and pepper to taste

Instructions:

1. In a large pan, heat the olive oil over medium heat. Add the

chopped onion and garlic and cook
until the onion is translucent.

2. Add the Arborio rice to the pan
   and stir to coat the rice with the
   oil. Cook for 1-2 minutes.

3. Add the vegetable broth, smoked
   paprika, and saffron threads to the
   pan. Stir to combine and bring to a
   boil.

4. Reduce the heat to low and add
   the artichoke hearts, peas, and
   sliced red bell pepper to the pan.
   Cover and cook for 15-20 minutes,
   or until the rice is cooked through
   and the vegetables are tender.

5. Season with salt and pepper to
   taste. Serve hot.

Greek Briam (Roasted Vegetables with Feta and Oregano)

Ingredients:

- 2 large potatoes, peeled and sliced
- 2 zucchinis, sliced
- 2 eggplants, sliced
- 2 red bell peppers, sliced
- 1 onion, sliced
- 4 cloves garlic, minced
- 1/4 cup olive oil
- 1 tsp dried oregano
- Salt and pepper to taste
- 1/2 cup crumbled feta cheese

Instructions:

1. Preheat the oven to 375°F (190°C).
2. In a large bowl, combine the sliced potatoes, zucchinis, eggplants, red

bell peppers, onion, and minced garlic.

3. Drizzle the olive oil over the vegetables and sprinkle with dried oregano, salt, and pepper. Toss to coat.

4. Transfer the vegetables to a large baking dish and spread them out evenly.

5. Bake in the preheated oven for 45-60 minutes, or until the vegetables are tender and lightly browned.

6. Remove from the oven and sprinkle the crumbled feta cheese over the top of the vegetables. Return to the oven and bake for an additional 10-15 minutes, or until the cheese is melted and bubbly.

7. Serve hot, garnished with additional oregano if desired.

Italian Spaghetti with Roasted Cherry Tomatoes and Garlic

Ingredients:

- 1 pound spaghetti
- 1 pint cherry tomatoes
- 4 cloves garlic, minced
- 1/4 cup olive oil
- Salt and pepper to taste
- Grated Parmesan cheese for serving

Instructions:

1. Preheat the oven to 400°F (200°C).

2. Spread the cherry tomatoes and minced garlic on a baking sheet. Drizzle with olive oil and season with salt and pepper.

3. Roast in the preheated oven for 20-25 minutes, or until the tomatoes are soft and slightly browned.

4. While the tomatoes are roasting, cook the spaghetti according to the package directions until al dente.

5. Drain the spaghetti and return it to the pot. Add the roasted cherry tomatoes and garlic, along with any oil and juices from the baking sheet.

6. Toss the spaghetti with the tomato mixture to combine.

7. Serve hot, garnished with grated Parmesan cheese.

Turkish Imam Bayildi (Stuffed Eggplant with Tomato Sauce and Garlic Yogurt)

Ingredients:

- 4 medium-sized eggplants
- 1 onion, chopped
- 3 cloves garlic, minced
- 2 tomatoes, chopped
- 2 tbsp tomato paste
- 1/2 cup water
- 2 tbsp olive oil
- Salt and pepper to taste
- 1/4 cup chopped parsley for garnish

For the garlic yogurt sauce:

- 1 cup plain Greek yogurt
- 2 cloves garlic, minced
- 1/2 tsp salt
- 1 tbsp chopped fresh mint (optional)

Instructions:

1. Preheat the oven to 400°F (200°C).
2. Cut off the stem of each eggplant, and slice them in half lengthwise.
3. Using a spoon, scoop out the flesh of the eggplants, leaving a 1/4-inch thick shell. Reserve the flesh and chop it into small pieces.
4. In a large pan, heat the olive oil over medium heat. Add the

chopped onion and garlic and cook until the onion is translucent.

5. Add the chopped eggplant flesh, chopped tomatoes, tomato paste, water, salt, and pepper to the pan. Stir to combine and bring to a boil.

6. Reduce the heat to low and simmer for 10-15 minutes, or until the vegetables are tender and the sauce has thickened.

7. Fill each eggplant shell with the tomato mixture and arrange them in a baking dish.

8. Cover the dish with foil and bake in the preheated oven for 30-40 minutes, or until the eggplants are tender.

9. While the eggplants are baking, prepare the garlic yogurt sauce. In

a small bowl, combine the Greek yogurt, minced garlic, salt, and chopped mint (if using). Stir to combine.

10. Serve the stuffed eggplants hot, garnished with chopped parsley and a dollop of garlic yogurt sauce.

Section 4: Sides and Accompaniments

Greek Salad with Feta Cheese

Ingredients:

- 1 large cucumber, chopped
- 2 large tomatoes, chopped
- 1 red onion, sliced
- 1 green bell pepper, sliced
- 1/2 cup kalamata olives
- 1/2 cup crumbled feta cheese
- 1/4 cup chopped fresh parsley
- 2 tablespoons red wine vinegar
- 1/4 cup olive oil
- Salt and black pepper to taste

Instructions:

1. In a large mixing bowl, combine cucumber, tomato, red onion, bell pepper, and olives.
2. Sprinkle feta cheese and parsley over the top of the mixture.
3. Drizzle with red wine vinegar and olive oil, then season with salt and black pepper to taste.
4. Toss everything together until evenly combined.
5. Serve chilled.

Roasted Eggplant Dip (Baba Ghanoush)

Ingredients:

- 1 large eggplant
- 1/4 cup tahini
- 2 cloves garlic, minced

- 2 tablespoons lemon juice
- 1/4 cup olive oil
- Salt and black pepper to taste

Instructions:

1. Preheat your oven to 400°F (205°C).
2. Pierce the eggplant all over with a fork, then place it on a baking sheet.
3. Roast the eggplant in the preheated oven for 30-40 minutes, or until it is very tender and the skin is charred.
4. Allow the eggplant to cool, then peel off the skin and discard it.
5. Place the roasted eggplant flesh in a food processor or blender.

6. Add tahini, garlic, lemon juice, olive oil, salt, and black pepper.

7. Process everything until the mixture is smooth and creamy.

8. Transfer the dip to a serving bowl and chill for at least 30 minutes before serving.

9. Drizzle with additional olive oil and sprinkle with fresh herbs (such as parsley or mint) if desired.

Marinated Olives with Garlic and Herbs

Ingredients:

- 2 cups mixed olives (such as kalamata, green, and black)
- 2 cloves garlic, sliced

- 2 tablespoons chopped fresh herbs (such as thyme, rosemary, or oregano)
- 1/4 cup olive oil
- 1 tablespoon lemon zest
- Salt and black pepper to taste

Instructions:

- In a large mixing bowl, combine olives, garlic, and herbs.
- In a separate small bowl, whisk together olive oil, lemon zest, salt, and black pepper.
- Pour the olive oil mixture over the olives and toss until everything is well coated.
- Cover the bowl with plastic wrap and refrigerate for at least 30 minutes before serving.

- Serve chilled, with toothpicks for easy snacking.

Spinach and Feta Stuffed Mushrooms

Ingredients:

- 16 large button mushrooms, stems removed
- 1 cup chopped fresh spinach
- 1/2 cup crumbled feta cheese
- 2 cloves garlic, minced
- 1/4 cup chopped fresh parsley
- 2 tablespoons olive oil
- Salt and black pepper to taste

Instructions:

1. Preheat your oven to 375°F (190°C).

2. In a large mixing bowl, combine chopped spinach, feta cheese, garlic, parsley, and olive oil.

3. Season the mixture with salt and black pepper to taste.

4. Use a spoon to fill each mushroom cap with a generous amount of the spinach and feta filling.

5. Place the stuffed mushrooms on a baking sheet lined with parchment paper.

6. Bake in the preheated oven for 20-25 minutes, or until the mushrooms are tender and the filling is hot and bubbly.

7. Serve the stuffed mushrooms immediately as a delicious and hearty vegetarian appetizer or side dish.

Roasted Tomatoes with Garlic and Basil

Ingredients:

- 4-6 ripe tomatoes, halved
- 4 cloves garlic, minced
- 1/4 cup fresh basil, chopped
- 2 tablespoons olive oil
- Salt and pepper to taste

Instructions:

1. Preheat the oven to 375°F.
2. Cut the tomatoes in half and place them in a baking dish, cut side up.
3. In a small bowl, mix together the minced garlic, chopped basil, and olive oil.

4. Spoon the garlic and basil mixture evenly over the tomato halves.
5. Sprinkle salt and pepper over the top of the tomatoes.
6. Roast in the oven for 20-25 minutes, until the tomatoes are soft and slightly caramelized.
7. Serve hot or at room temperature as a side dish or accompaniment.

Grilled Zucchini with Lemon and Mint

Ingredients:

- 2-3 medium zucchinis, sliced lengthwise
- 1/4 cup olive oil
- Juice of 1 lemon

- 2 tablespoons fresh mint leaves, chopped
- Salt and pepper to taste

Instructions:

1. Preheat a grill or grill pan to medium-high heat.
2. Brush the sliced zucchini with olive oil on both sides.
3. Grill the zucchini for 3-4 minutes on each side, until lightly charred and tender.
4. Remove the zucchini from the grill and place on a serving platter.
5. Drizzle the lemon juice over the grilled zucchini.
6. Sprinkle the chopped mint over the top of the zucchini.

7. Season with salt and pepper to taste.

8. Serve hot as a side dish or accompaniment.

Couscous Salad with Roasted Vegetables

Ingredients:

- 1 cup couscous
- 2 cups vegetable broth or water
- 1 medium eggplant, diced
- 1 red bell pepper, diced
- 1 yellow onion, diced
- 2 tablespoons olive oil
- 2 tablespoons fresh parsley, chopped
- Salt and pepper to taste

Instructions:

1. Preheat the oven to 400°F.

2. In a large bowl, toss the diced eggplant, red bell pepper, and onion with olive oil.

3. Spread the vegetables out on a baking sheet and roast in the oven for 25-30 minutes, until they are tender and slightly charred.

4. While the vegetables are roasting, prepare the couscous according to the package instructions, using vegetable broth or water.

5. Once the couscous is cooked, fluff it with a fork and transfer it to a large bowl.

6. Add the roasted vegetables to the bowl with the couscous and mix well.

7. Sprinkle chopped parsley over the top of the couscous and vegetables.

8. Season with salt and pepper to taste.

9. Serve hot, cold, or at room temperature as a side dish or accompaniment.

Hummus with Roasted Red Peppers

Ingredients:

- 1 can chickpeas, drained and rinsed
- 1/4 cup tahini
- 1/4 cup lemon juice
- 2-3 cloves garlic, minced
- 1/4 cup olive oil

- 1/4 cup roasted red peppers, chopped
- Salt and pepper to taste

Instructions:

1. In a food processor, combine the chickpeas, tahini, lemon juice, and minced garlic.
2. Process until the mixture is smooth, scraping down the sides of the food processor as needed.
3. While the food processor is running, slowly pour in the olive oil and blend until the mixture is creamy.
4. Add the chopped roasted red peppers to the mixture and pulse a few times until well combined.

5. Season the hummus with salt and pepper to taste.

6. Transfer the hummus to a serving bowl and garnish with additional chopped roasted red peppers and a drizzle of olive oil.

7. Serve the hummus with pita bread, crackers, or fresh vegetables as a side dish or accompaniment.

Mediterranean Quinoa Salad with Feta and Olives

Ingredients:

- 1 cup quinoa, rinsed and drained
- 2 cups vegetable broth or water
- 1 medium cucumber, diced
- 1 pint cherry tomatoes, halved

- 1/2 cup kalamata olives, pitted and chopped
- 1/2 cup crumbled feta cheese
- 1/4 cup red onion, finely chopped
- 2 tablespoons fresh parsley, chopped
- 2 tablespoons fresh mint, chopped
- 1/4 cup olive oil
- 2 tablespoons red wine vinegar
- Salt and pepper to taste

Instructions:

1. In a medium saucepan, combine the quinoa and vegetable broth or water.
2. Bring the mixture to a boil, then reduce the heat to low and simmer for 15-20 minutes, until the quinoa

is cooked and the liquid is absorbed.

3. Fluff the quinoa with a fork and transfer it to a large bowl.

4. Add the diced cucumber, halved cherry tomatoes, chopped kalamata olives, crumbled feta cheese, finely chopped red onion, chopped parsley, and chopped mint to the bowl with the quinoa.

5. In a small bowl, whisk together the olive oil, red wine vinegar, salt, and pepper.

6. Pour the dressing over the quinoa salad and mix well.

7. Serve the quinoa salad cold or at room temperature as a side dish or accompaniment.

Roasted Garlic and Chickpea Dip (Hummus)

Ingredients:

- 1 can of chickpeas, drained and rinsed
- 1 head of garlic
- 1/4 cup tahini
- 1/4 cup lemon juice
- 2 tablespoons olive oil
- Salt and pepper to taste

Instructions:

1. Preheat the oven to 400°F.
2. Cut off the top of the head of garlic to expose the cloves. Drizzle with olive oil and wrap in foil.
3. Roast the garlic in the oven for 30-40 minutes or until the cloves are soft and caramelized.

4. In a food processor, blend the chickpeas, tahini, lemon juice, and olive oil until smooth.
5. Squeeze the roasted garlic cloves into the food processor and blend until well combined.
6. Season with salt and pepper to taste.
7. Serve with pita chips, sliced veggies, or use as a spread on sandwiches.

Tabbouleh Salad with Bulgur Wheat and Parsley

Ingredients:
- 1 cup bulgur wheat
- 1 1/2 cups boiling water
- 1/4 cup lemon juice

- 1/4 cup olive oil
- 1 garlic clove, minced
- 1/2 teaspoon salt
- 1/4 teaspoon black pepper
- 1 cup chopped fresh parsley
- 1/2 cup chopped fresh mint
- 2 tomatoes, seeded and diced
- 1 cucumber, peeled, seeded and diced
- 1/2 red onion, diced

Instructions:

1. In a medium bowl, combine bulgur wheat and boiling water. Cover and let stand for 30 minutes.
2. In a small bowl, whisk together lemon juice, olive oil, garlic, salt, and pepper.

3. Fluff the bulgur wheat with a fork and add parsley, mint, tomatoes, cucumber, and red onion. Toss to combine.
4. Pour the dressing over the salad and toss again to coat.
5. Chill in the refrigerator for at least 30 minutes before serving.

Roasted Red Pepper and Tomato Soup

Ingredients:
- 2 red bell peppers, halved and seeded
- 2 tablespoons olive oil
- 1 onion, chopped
- 2 garlic cloves, minced
- 1 can diced tomatoes

- 1 tablespoon tomato paste
- 1 teaspoon smoked paprika
- 1/2 teaspoon dried oregano
- 3 cups vegetable broth
- Salt and pepper to taste

Instructions:

1. Preheat the broiler to high.
2. Place the bell pepper halves on a baking sheet and broil until charred, about 10 minutes.
3. Remove from the oven and place the peppers in a paper bag. Close the bag and let the peppers steam for 10 minutes.
4. Peel the skin off the peppers and chop into small pieces.
5. In a large pot, heat the olive oil over medium heat. Add the onion

and garlic and sauté until softened, about 5 minutes.

6. Add the diced tomatoes, tomato paste, smoked paprika, oregano, and chopped red peppers. Stir to combine.

7. Pour in the vegetable broth and bring to a boil. Reduce the heat and simmer for 20 minutes.

8. Use an immersion blender or transfer to a blender and blend until smooth.

9. Season with salt and pepper to taste.

Mediterranean Stuffed Peppers with Rice and Feta Cheese

Ingredients:

- 4 bell peppers, halved and seeded
- 1 cup cooked rice
- 1/2 cup crumbled feta cheese
- 1/4 cup chopped fresh parsley
- 1/4 cup chopped fresh mint
- 1/4 cup chopped sun-dried tomatoes
- 1/4 cup chopped kalamata olives
- 2 tablespoons olive oil
- 1 garlic clove, minced
- Salt and pepper to taste

Instructions:

1. Preheat the oven to 375°F.
2. In a large bowl, mix together the cooked rice, feta cheese, parsley, mint, sun-dried tomatoes, kalamata olives, olive oil, garlic, salt, and pepper.

3. Stuff each pepper half with the rice mixture, packing it tightly.
4. Place the stuffed peppers in a baking dish and cover with foil.
5. Bake for 30-35 minutes or until the peppers are tender.
6. Remove the foil and bake for an additional 10 minutes to brown the tops of the peppers.
7. Serve hot as a main dish or side dish. Optional: garnish with additional chopped parsley and mint.

Grilled Artichokes with Lemon and Garlic

Ingredients:

- 4 large artichokes
- 1/4 cup olive oil
- 4 cloves garlic, minced
- Juice of 1 lemon
- Salt and pepper, to taste

Instructions:

1. Preheat grill to medium-high heat.
2. Cut off the top 1/3 of each artichoke and trim the stem.
3. Use a spoon to scoop out the fuzzy choke from the center of each artichoke.
4. In a small bowl, whisk together olive oil, garlic, lemon juice, salt, and pepper.

5. Brush the artichokes generously with the garlic and lemon mixture.
6. Grill the artichokes for 15-20 minutes, turning occasionally, until they are tender and lightly charred.
7. Serve hot with additional lemon wedges.

Greek Roasted Potatoes with Lemon and Oregano

Ingredients:

- 2 lbs. potatoes, cut into bite-size pieces
- 1/4 cup olive oil
- 2 cloves garlic, minced
- Juice of 1 lemon
- 1 tsp. dried oregano

- Salt and pepper, to taste

Instructions:

1. Preheat oven to 400°F.
2. In a large bowl, whisk together olive oil, garlic, lemon juice, oregano, salt, and pepper.
3. Add the potatoes to the bowl and toss to coat evenly with the olive oil mixture.
4. Spread the potatoes out in a single layer on a baking sheet.
5. Roast the potatoes for 25-30 minutes, stirring occasionally, until they are golden brown and crispy on the outside and tender on the inside.
6. Serve hot with additional lemon wedges.

Grilled Halloumi Cheese with Watermelon and Mint

Ingredients:

- 1 lb. halloumi cheese, sliced
- 2 cups watermelon, diced
- 1/4 cup fresh mint leaves, chopped
- 2 tbsp. olive oil
- Juice of 1 lime
- Salt and pepper, to taste

Instructions:

1. Preheat grill to medium-high heat.
2. In a large bowl, whisk together olive oil, lime juice, salt, and pepper.

3. Add the watermelon and mint to the bowl and toss to coat evenly with the olive oil mixture.
4. Grill the halloumi cheese for 2-3 minutes per side, until it is lightly charred and softened.
5. Arrange the grilled halloumi cheese on a platter and top with the watermelon and mint mixture.
6. Serve immediately.

Grilled Vegetables with Balsamic Glaze

Ingredients:
- 2 zucchinis, sliced
- 2 bell peppers, sliced
- 1 red onion, sliced
- 1/4 cup olive oil

- Salt and pepper, to taste
- 1/4 cup balsamic vinegar
- 2 tbsp. honey

Instructions:

1. Preheat grill to medium-high heat.
2. In a large bowl, toss the zucchini, bell peppers, and red onion with olive oil, salt, and pepper.
3. Grill the vegetables for 10-12 minutes, turning occasionally, until they are lightly charred and tender.
4. In a small saucepan, whisk together balsamic vinegar and honey.
5. Heat the mixture over medium heat for 5-7 minutes, stirring

frequently, until it has thickened and reduced by about half.

6. Drizzle the balsamic glaze over the grilled vegetables and serve hot.

Fattoush Salad with Pita Chips and Sumac

Ingredients:

- 1 large head romaine lettuce, chopped
- 1 cup cherry tomatoes, halved
- 1 cup cucumber, diced
- 1/2 cup red onion, thinly sliced
- 1/4 cup fresh parsley, chopped
- 1/4 cup fresh mint, chopped
- 1/4 cup olive oil
- 2 tbsp lemon juice
- 1 clove garlic, minced

- 1 tsp sumac
- Salt and pepper to taste
- 2 pita breads, cut into small pieces and toasted

Instructions:

1. Preheat your oven to 375°F.
2. Cut the pita bread into small pieces and spread them out on a baking sheet. Toast in the oven for 5-7 minutes, or until crispy.
3. In a large mixing bowl, combine the chopped romaine lettuce, cherry tomatoes, diced cucumber, sliced red onion, chopped parsley, and chopped mint.
4. In a separate small mixing bowl, whisk together the olive oil, lemon

juice, minced garlic, sumac, and a pinch of salt and pepper.

5. Pour the dressing over the salad and toss to combine.

6. Add the toasted pita chips to the salad and give it another toss.

7. Serve immediately and enjoy your delicious and refreshing Fattoush Salad with Pita Chips and Sumac!

Roasted Beet Salad with Feta Cheese and Walnuts

Ingredients:

- 4 medium beets, washed and trimmed
- 2 tbsp olive oil
- Salt and pepper to taste
- 4 cups mixed greens

- 1/2 cup crumbled feta cheese
- 1/4 cup chopped walnuts
- 1 tbsp balsamic vinegar
- 1 tbsp honey
- 1 tsp Dijon mustard
- 1/4 cup olive oil

Instructions:

1. Preheat your oven to 400°F.
2. Wash and trim the beets, then wrap them in foil and place them on a baking sheet. Roast in the oven for 40-45 minutes, or until tender.
3. Once the beets are cool enough to handle, remove the skins and chop them into bite-sized pieces.
4. In a large mixing bowl, combine the mixed greens, chopped beets,

crumbled feta cheese, and chopped walnuts.

5.

6. In a separate small mixing bowl, whisk together the balsamic vinegar, honey, Dijon mustard, and olive oil. Season with salt and pepper to taste.

7. Pour the dressing over the salad and toss to combine.

8. Serve immediately and enjoy your tasty and nutritious Roasted Beet Salad with Feta Cheese and Walnuts!

Mediterranean Baked Sweet Potatoes with Chickpeas and Tahini Sauce

Ingredients:

- 2 large sweet potatoes, washed and scrubbed
- 1 tbsp olive oil
- Salt and pepper to taste
- 1 can chickpeas, drained and rinsed
- 1 tsp smoked paprika
- 1/2 tsp garlic powder
- 1/2 tsp onion powder
- 1/2 tsp cumin
- 1/4 tsp cayenne pepper
- 1/4 cup tahini
- 1/4 cup lemon juice
- 1/4 cup water

- 1 clove garlic, minced
- Salt and pepper to taste
- Fresh parsley for garnish

Instructions:

1. Preheat your oven to 400°F.
2. Cut the sweet potatoes in half lengthwise and place them cut-side up on a baking sheet.
3. Brush the sweet potatoes with olive oil and season with salt and pepper to taste.
4. Roast the sweet potatoes in the oven for 30-35 minutes, or until tender.
5. While the sweet potatoes are roasting, prepare the chickpeas. In a small bowl, mix together the smoked paprika, garlic powder,

onion powder, cumin, and cayenne pepper.

6. In a separate mixing bowl, toss the chickpeas with the spice mixture until they are evenly coated.

7. Once the sweet potatoes are done, remove them from the oven and top each one with a portion of the spiced chickpeas.

8. Return the sweet potatoes to the oven and bake for an additional 5-10 minutes, or until the chickpeas are heated through.

9. While the sweet potatoes are finishing up, prepare the tahini sauce. In a small mixing bowl, whisk together the tahini, lemon juice, water, minced garlic, and a pinch of salt and pepper.

10. Remove the sweet potatoes from the oven and drizzle them with the tahini sauce.

11. Garnish with fresh parsley and serve immediately.

Enjoy your delicious and satisfying Mediterranean Baked Sweet Potatoes with Chickpeas and Tahini Sauce!

Section 5: Desserts

Greek Yogurt and Honey Parfait Recipe

Ingredients:

- 2 cups Greek yogurt
- 1/4 cup honey
- 1 tsp vanilla extract
- 1 cup mixed berries (strawberries, raspberries, blueberries)
- 1/4 cup granola
- Fresh mint leaves (optional)

Instructions:

1. In a mixing bowl, combine the Greek yogurt, honey, and vanilla extract until well blended.

2. Take 4 serving glasses and spoon a layer of the yogurt mixture into the bottom of each glass.

3. Add a layer of mixed berries on top of the yogurt layer.

4. Spoon another layer of yogurt mixture on top of the berries.

5. Add another layer of berries on top of the yogurt layer.

6. Finish by sprinkling the granola on top of each glass.

7. Garnish with fresh mint leaves if desired.

8. Chill in the refrigerator for at least 30 minutes before serving.

Baklava with Walnuts and Honey Recipe

Ingredients:

- 1 package phyllo dough
- 1 cup walnuts, chopped
- 1/2 cup unsalted butter, melted
- 1/2 cup honey
- 1/2 cup water
- 1/2 tsp ground cinnamon

Instructions:

1. Preheat the oven to 350°F (180°C).
2. In a mixing bowl, combine the chopped walnuts and ground cinnamon.
3. Grease a baking dish with some of the melted butter.

4. Place a sheet of phyllo dough on the bottom of the baking dish and brush it with melted butter.

5. Add another sheet of phyllo dough on top and brush with melted butter.

6. Continue layering the phyllo dough, brushing each sheet with melted butter, until half of the phyllo dough has been used.

7. Spread the walnut and cinnamon mixture evenly over the phyllo dough.

8. Continue layering the remaining phyllo dough on top of the walnut mixture, brushing each sheet with melted butter.

9. Using a sharp knife, score the top layer of phyllo dough into diamond-shaped pieces.

10. Bake in the oven for 25-30 minutes, or until golden brown.

11. While the baklava is baking, make the syrup by combining the honey and water in a saucepan and heating over medium heat until the honey is dissolved.

12. Remove the baklava from the oven and immediately pour the syrup over the top.

13. Allow the baklava to cool and absorb the syrup before serving.

Fig and Almond Tart Recipe

Ingredients:

- 1 ready-made pie crust
- 1/2 cup almond meal
- 1/4 cup granulated sugar
- 1/4 cup unsalted butter, melted
- 1 egg
- 5-6 ripe figs, sliced

Instructions:

1. Preheat the oven to 375°F (190°C).
2. In a mixing bowl, combine the almond meal, granulated sugar, melted butter, and egg until well blended.
3. Roll out the pie crust and place it in a tart pan.
4. Pour the almond mixture into the pie crust and spread it evenly.
5. Arrange the sliced figs on top of the almond mixture.

6. Bake in the oven for 25-30 minutes, or until the crust is golden brown and the filling is set.
7. Allow the tart to cool before slicing and serving.

Orange and Olive Oil Cake Recipe

Ingredients:

- 2 oranges
- 3 eggs
- 1/2 cup granulated sugar
- 1/2 cup olive oil
- 1 cup all-purpose flour
- 1 tsp baking powder
- Powdered sugar for dusting (optional)

Instructions:

1. Preheat the oven to 350°F (180°C).

2. Cut the oranges into quarters, remove any seeds, and puree them in a blender or food processor until smooth.

3. In a mixing bowl, beat the eggs and granulated sugar together until light and fluffy.

4. Slowly add in the olive oil and continue to beat until well blended.

5. In a separate bowl, whisk together the flour and baking powder.

6. Gradually add the dry ingredients to the egg mixture and mix until well combined.

7. Fold in the orange puree until well incorporated.

8. Grease a 9-inch cake pan with olive oil and pour the batter into the pan.

9. Bake in the oven for 40-45 minutes, or until a toothpick inserted into the center comes out clean.

10. Allow the cake to cool in the pan for 10 minutes before removing and placing it on a wire rack to cool completely.

11. Dust with powdered sugar before serving (optional).

Roasted Apricots with Yogurt and Honey Recipe

Ingredients:

- 6 ripe apricots
- 1/4 cup plain Greek yogurt
- 1 tablespoon honey
- 1/4 teaspoon ground cinnamon
- 1/4 cup sliced almonds

Instructions:

1. Preheat the oven to 375°F (190°C). Line a baking sheet with parchment paper.
2. Cut the apricots in half and remove the pits.
3. Place the apricot halves on the prepared baking sheet, cut-side up.

4. In a small bowl, mix the Greek yogurt, honey, and cinnamon until well combined.
5. Spoon the yogurt mixture onto each apricot half, spreading it out evenly.
6. Sprinkle the sliced almonds over the top of the yogurt mixture.
7. Bake in the preheated oven for 15-20 minutes, or until the apricots are soft and the yogurt mixture is lightly browned.
8. Serve warm or at room temperature.

Enjoy your delicious and healthy Roasted Apricots with Yogurt and Honey!

Note: You can also try using other fruits like peaches or plums in place of apricots for variation.

Tahini and Almond Cookies

Ingredients:

- 1 cup almond flour
- 1/2 cup tahini
- 1/4 cup maple syrup
- 1 tsp vanilla extract
- 1/4 tsp sea salt
- 1/4 tsp baking soda

Instructions:

1. Preheat the oven to 350°F (180°C). Line a baking sheet with parchment paper.

2. In a mixing bowl, combine almond flour, tahini, maple syrup, vanilla extract, sea salt, and baking soda.

3. Mix all the ingredients together until a smooth dough forms.

4. Scoop dough by tablespoonfuls and place them on the prepared baking sheet.

5. Use a fork to flatten each cookie slightly.

6. Bake for 10-12 minutes or until the edges are lightly golden brown.

7. Remove from the oven and let cool on the baking sheet for 5 minutes.

8. Transfer the cookies to a wire rack to cool completely.

9. Serve and enjoy!

Pistachio and Honey Cake

Ingredients:

- 1 cup all-purpose flour
- 1/2 cup pistachios, ground
- 1/2 cup honey
- 1/4 cup vegetable oil
- 2 large eggs
- 1/2 tsp baking powder
- 1/4 tsp baking soda
- 1/4 tsp salt
- 1/2 cup plain Greek yogurt
- 1/4 cup pistachios, chopped (for garnish)

Instructions:

1. Preheat the oven to 350°F (180°C). Grease a 9-inch cake pan with cooking spray and line the bottom with parchment paper.

2. In a mixing bowl, whisk together the all-purpose flour, ground pistachios, baking powder, baking soda, and salt.

3. In another mixing bowl, whisk together the honey, vegetable oil, and eggs until smooth.

4. Add the dry ingredients to the wet ingredients and mix until just combined.

5. Add the Greek yogurt and mix until smooth.

6. Pour the batter into the prepared cake pan.

7. Sprinkle the chopped pistachios on top of the batter.

8. Bake for 25-30 minutes or until a toothpick inserted into the center of the cake comes out clean.

9. Remove from the oven and let cool for 10 minutes.

10. Run a knife around the edges of the cake pan to loosen the cake, then transfer to a wire rack to cool completely.

11. Serve and enjoy!

Greek Yogurt and Mixed Berry Popsicles

Ingredients:

- 2 cups plain Greek yogurt
- 1 cup mixed berries (fresh or frozen)
- 1/4 cup honey

Instructions:

1. In a blender, puree the mixed berries until smooth.
2. In a mixing bowl, whisk together the Greek yogurt and honey until smooth.
3. Add the pureed berries to the Greek yogurt mixture and stir until well combined.
4. Pour the mixture into popsicle molds.
5. Freeze for at least 4 hours or until firm.
6. To remove the popsicles from the molds, run the molds under warm water for a few seconds to loosen.
7. Serve and enjoy!

Chocolate Olive Oil Cake

Ingredients:

- 1 1/2 cups all-purpose flour
- 1/2 cup unsweetened cocoa powder
- 1 tsp baking soda
- 1/2 tsp salt
- 1 cup granulated sugar
- 3/4 cup extra-virgin olive oil
- 1 cup water
- 1 tbsp white vinegar
- 1 tsp vanilla extract
- Powdered sugar (optional)

Instructions:

1. Preheat the oven to 350°F (175°C). Grease an 8-inch round cake pan with olive oil or cooking spray.

2. In a medium bowl, whisk together the flour, cocoa powder, baking soda, and salt.

3. In a large bowl, whisk together the sugar, olive oil, water, vinegar, and vanilla extract until well combined.

4. Gradually add the dry ingredients to the wet ingredients, stirring until just combined.

5. Pour the batter into the prepared cake pan and bake for 30-35 minutes, or until a toothpick inserted into the center of the cake comes out clean.

6. Allow the cake to cool in the pan for 10 minutes before removing it and transferring it to a wire rack to cool completely.

7. Once cooled, dust the top of the cake with powdered sugar (optional) and slice into wedges.

Greek Honey and Sesame Seed Candy

Ingredients:

- 1 cup sesame seeds
- 1/2 cup honey
- 1/2 cup sugar
- 1/2 tsp cinnamon
- 1/4 tsp sea salt

Instructions:

1. Preheat the oven to 350°F (175°C). Spread the sesame seeds out on a baking sheet and toast in the oven

for 10-12 minutes, or until golden brown.

2. In a medium saucepan, combine the honey, sugar, cinnamon, and salt over medium heat. Stir until the sugar is dissolved.

3. Add the toasted sesame seeds to the saucepan and stir until well combined.

4. Pour the mixture into a greased 8-inch square baking dish and use a spatula to smooth it out.

5. Let the candy cool at room temperature for at least 1 hour, or until firm.

6. Cut the candy into small squares or rectangles and serve.

Quince and Almond Tart

Ingredients:

- 1 1/2 cups all-purpose flour
- 1/4 cup almond flour
- 1/4 tsp salt
- 1/2 cup unsalted butter, softened
- 1/4 cup granulated sugar
- 1 large egg yolk
- 1 tbsp cold water
- 3-4 ripe quinces, peeled, cored, and thinly sliced
- 1/2 cup honey
- 1/2 cup almond slivers

Instructions:

1. Preheat the oven to 375°F (190°C). Grease a 9-inch tart pan with a removable bottom.

2. In a medium bowl, whisk together the all-purpose flour, almond flour, and salt.

3. In a large bowl, beat the butter and sugar together until light and fluffy.

4. Add the egg yolk and water to the butter mixture and beat until well combined.

5. Gradually add the dry ingredients to the wet ingredients, stirring until the mixture forms a dough.

6. Roll out the dough on a floured surface and transfer it to the prepared tart pan.

7. Arrange the quince slices in an even layer over the dough.

8. Drizzle the honey over the quinces and sprinkle the almond slivers on top.

9. Bake the tart for 40-45 minutes, or until the crust is golden brown and the quinces are tender.

10.   10. Let the tart cool in the pan for at least 15 minutes before removing it from the pan and slicing it into wedges.

Baked Figs with Goat Cheese and Honey

Ingredients:
- 8 fresh figs, halved
- 1/2 cup crumbled goat cheese
- 2 tbsp honey
- 1/4 tsp sea salt

- Freshly ground black pepper

Instructions:

1. Preheat the oven to 375°F (190°C). Line a baking sheet with parchment paper.
2. Arrange the fig halves on the baking sheet, cut side up.
3. Sprinkle the crumbled goat cheese over the figs.
4. Drizzle the honey over the goat cheese and figs.
5. Sprinkle the sea salt and black pepper over the top.
6. Bake the figs for 12-15 minutes, or until the cheese is melted and bubbly.
7. Serve the baked figs warm as a dessert or appetizer.

Almond and Orange Blossom Cookies

Ingredients:

- 1 cup almond flour
- 1/2 cup all-purpose flour
- 1/2 cup sugar
- 1/2 tsp baking powder
- 1/4 tsp salt
- 1/4 cup olive oil
- 1 egg
- 1 tsp vanilla extract
- 1 tsp orange blossom water
- 1/4 cup sliced almonds

Directions:

1. Preheat the oven to 350°F (180°C).

2. In a large mixing bowl, whisk together the almond flour, all-purpose flour, sugar, baking powder, and salt.
3. Add the olive oil, egg, vanilla extract, and orange blossom water to the dry ingredients and mix until well combined.
4. Use a cookie scoop or spoon to drop spoonfuls of the dough onto a baking sheet lined with parchment paper.
5. Sprinkle the sliced almonds over the top of the cookies.
6. Bake for 12-15 minutes, or until the edges of the cookies are golden brown.
7. Remove from the oven and let cool on the baking sheet for 5 minutes

before transferring to a wire rack to cool completely.

8. Enjoy your delicious Almond and Orange Blossom Cookies!

Spiced Apple and Almond Cake

Ingredients:

- 1/2 cup unsalted butter, softened
- 1/2 cup sugar
- 2 eggs
- 1 tsp vanilla extract
- 1 1/2 cups all-purpose flour
- 1 tsp baking powder
- 1/2 tsp ground cinnamon
- 1/4 tsp ground ginger
- 1/4 tsp ground nutmeg
- 1/4 tsp salt
- 1/2 cup almond milk

- 2 medium apples, peeled and diced
- 1/2 cup sliced almonds

Directions:

1. Preheat the oven to 350°F (180°C). Grease a 9-inch round cake pan and set aside.
2. In a large mixing bowl, cream together the butter and sugar until light and fluffy.
3. Beat in the eggs one at a time, followed by the vanilla extract.
4. In a separate bowl, whisk together the flour, baking powder, cinnamon, ginger, nutmeg, and salt.
5. Add the dry ingredients to the butter mixture in three parts,

alternating with the almond milk and mixing until just combined.

6. Fold in the diced apples and sliced almonds.

7. Pour the batter into the prepared cake pan and smooth the top with a spatula.

8. Bake for 35-40 minutes, or until a toothpick inserted into the center of the cake comes out clean.

9. Remove from the oven and let cool in the pan for 10 minutes before transferring to a wire rack to cool completely.

10. Serve and enjoy your Spiced Apple and Almond Cake!

Lemon and Olive Oil Cake

Ingredients:

- 1 cup all-purpose flour
- 1/2 cup almond flour
- 1 tsp baking powder
- 1/4 tsp salt
- 3/4 cup sugar
- 2 large eggs
- 1/2 cup olive oil
- 1/2 cup almond milk
- 1/4 cup lemon juice
- 2 tbsp lemon zest
- 1/4 cup sliced almonds

Directions:

1. Preheat the oven to 350°F (180°C). Grease an 8-inch round cake pan and set aside.

2. In a medium mixing bowl, whisk together the all-purpose flour, almond flour, baking powder, and salt.

3. In a separate large mixing bowl, whisk together the sugar and eggs until pale and thick.

4. Slowly pour in the olive oil while whisking continuously until fully incorporated.

5. Add the dry ingredients to the wet mixture in three parts, alternating with the almond milk and mixing until just combined.

6. Mix in the lemon juice and lemon zest.

7. Pour the batter into the prepared cake pan and smooth the top with a spatula.

8. Sprinkle sliced almonds over the top of the cake.

9. Bake for 30-35 minutes, or until a toothpick inserted into the center of the cake comes out clean.

10. Remove from the oven and let cool in the pan for 10 minutes before transferring to a wire rack to cool completely.

11. Serve and enjoy your Lemon and Olive Oil Cake!

Semolina Halva with Pistachios

Ingredients:
- 1 cup semolina flour
- 1/2 cup unsalted butter
- 1 cup sugar
- 2 cups water

- 1/4 cup shelled pistachios, chopped
- 1/4 tsp ground cinnamon

Directions:

1. In a large saucepan, melt the butter over medium heat.
2. Add the semolina flour and stir continuously for 3-4 minutes, or until lightly browned and fragrant.
3. Add the sugar and water to the pan and stir until the sugar has dissolved.
4. Reduce the heat to low and simmer for 10-15 minutes, stirring occasionally, until the mixture has thickened and the semolina has absorbed most of the liquid.

5. Remove from the heat and stir in the chopped pistachios.

Transfer the mixture to a greased 9-inch square baking dish and smooth the top with a spatula.

Sprinkle cinnamon over the top of the mixture.

Let the mixture cool to room temperature and then refrigerate for at least 2 hours, or until set.

Cut into squares and serve chilled or at room temperature.

Enjoy your delicious Semolina Halva with Pistachios!

Greek Yogurt and Cherry Clafoutis

Ingredients:

- 1 cup Greek yogurt
- 1/2 cup all-purpose flour
- 1/2 cup granulated sugar
- 1/2 teaspoon baking powder
- 1/4 teaspoon salt
- 2 eggs
- 1 teaspoon vanilla extract
- 2 cups fresh cherries, pitted
- Powdered sugar, for dusting

Instructions:

1. Preheat the oven to 350°F (175°C). Grease a 9-inch pie dish with cooking spray.

2. In a large mixing bowl, whisk together the Greek yogurt, flour, sugar, baking powder, and salt until smooth.

3. Add the eggs and vanilla extract, and whisk until well combined.

4. Pour the batter into the prepared pie dish.

5. Scatter the pitted cherries over the top of the batter.

6. Bake for 35-40 minutes, or until the clafoutis is puffed and golden brown.

7. Remove from the oven and let cool for a few minutes before dusting with powdered sugar.

8. Serve warm or at room temperature.

Carrot and Pistachio Cake

Ingredients:

- 2 cups all-purpose flour

- 1 teaspoon baking soda
- 1 teaspoon baking powder
- 1/2 teaspoon salt
- 2 teaspoons ground cinnamon
- 1/4 teaspoon ground nutmeg
- 1/2 cup vegetable oil
- 1 cup granulated sugar
- 3 eggs
- 2 cups shredded carrots
- 1/2 cup chopped pistachios
- Cream cheese frosting (optional)

Instructions:

1. Preheat the oven to 350°F (175°C). Grease a 9-inch cake pan with cooking spray.
2. In a large mixing bowl, whisk together the flour, baking soda,

baking powder, salt, cinnamon, and nutmeg.

3. In a separate bowl, whisk together the vegetable oil, sugar, and eggs until smooth.

4. Add the wet ingredients to the dry ingredients, and stir until well combined.

5. Fold in the shredded carrots and chopped pistachios.

6. Pour the batter into the prepared cake pan.

7. Bake for 35-40 minutes, or until a toothpick inserted into the center of the cake comes out clean.

8. Let the cake cool completely before frosting with cream cheese frosting, if desired.

Chocolate and Hazelnut Baklava

Ingredients:

- 1 cup chopped hazelnuts
- 1/2 cup granulated sugar
- 1/2 teaspoon ground cinnamon
- 1/2 cup unsalted butter, melted
- 8 sheets phyllo dough
- 1/2 cup semisweet chocolate chips
- Honey, for drizzling

Instructions:

1. Preheat the oven to 350°F (175°C). Grease a 9-inch square baking dish with cooking spray.
2. In a mixing bowl, stir together the chopped hazelnuts, sugar, and cinnamon.
3. Brush the melted butter onto the bottom of the baking dish.

4. Lay 1 sheet of phyllo dough on top of the buttered baking dish, and brush it with butter.
5. Repeat with 3 more sheets of phyllo dough.
6. Sprinkle half of the hazelnut mixture over the phyllo dough.
7. Sprinkle the chocolate chips over the hazelnut mixture.
8. Repeat with another layer of phyllo dough and hazelnut mixture.
9. Top with the remaining 4 sheets of phyllo dough, brushing each sheet with butter.
10. Use a sharp knife to cut the baklava into squares.
11. Bake for 35-40 minutes, or until the top is golden brown and crisp.

12. Remove from the oven and let cool for a few minutes.

13. Drizzle honey over the top of the baklava.

14. Serve warm or at room temperaturc.

Stuffed Dates with Marzipan and Almonds

Ingredients:

- 12 medjool dates, pitted
- 1/2 cup marzipan
- 12 whole almonds
- Powdered sugar, for dusting

Instructions:

1. Preheat the oven to 350°F (175°C). Line a baking sheet with parchment paper.
2. Stuff each pitted date with a small amount of marzipan.
3. Place a whole almond in the center of each date.
4. Place the stuffed dates on the prepared baking sheet.
5. Bake for 10-12 minutes, or until the marzipan is golden brown and the dates are slightly caramelized.
6. Remove from the oven and let cool for a few minutes.
7. Dust with powdered sugar before serving.
8. Serve warm or at room temperature.

Conclusion

Tips for Eating a Mediterranean Vegetarian Diet

Incorporate a variety of colorful fruits and vegetables into your meals.

Use healthy fats like olive oil, avocado, and nuts in your cooking.

Include protein-rich plant-based foods such as legumes, nuts, seeds, and tofu.

Opt for whole grains like brown rice, quinoa, and whole-wheat pasta.

Flavor your meals with herbs and spices like basil, oregano, and cumin.

Use dairy products like yogurt and cheese in moderation.

Enjoy seafood in moderation, if desired.

Limit processed and refined foods, and avoid added sugars and saturated fats.

Glossary of Mediterranean Ingredients

Olive oil - a healthy monounsaturated fat used in cooking and dressings.

Tomatoes - a staple ingredient used in many Mediterranean dishes.

Garlic - a flavorful and aromatic bulb used to season dishes.

Chickpeas - a protein-rich legume commonly used in Mediterranean cuisine.

Feta cheese - a tangy and salty cheese made from sheep's milk.

Eggplant - a versatile vegetable commonly used in Mediterranean cooking.

Couscous - a small grain made from durum wheat that is often used in North African cuisine.

Lemon - a sour citrus fruit used to add flavor to many dishes.

Oregano - an herb commonly used in Mediterranean cuisine.

Dates - a sweet fruit commonly used in desserts and as a natural sweetener.

30-Day Meal Plan

Day 1:

- Breakfast: Mediterranean Veggie Omelette with tomatoes, spinach, and olives.

- Lunch: Greek Chickpea Salad with cucumbers, red onions, and feta cheese.

- Dinner: Eggplant Parmesan with a side of Quinoa Tabbouleh.

Day 2:

- Breakfast: Chia Seed Pudding with mixed berries and sliced almonds.

- Lunch: Mediterranean Lentil Soup with a side of whole-grain bread.

- Dinner: Stuffed Bell Peppers with a filling of couscous, pine nuts, and dried fruits.

Day 3:

- Breakfast: Greek Yogurt Parfait with granola, honey, and fresh fruit.
- Lunch: Falafel Pita with hummus, lettuce, and tomatoes.
- Dinner: Spanakopita - Greek Spinach Pie with a side of Greek Salad.

Day 4:

- Breakfast: Vegan Greek Yogurt with sliced peaches and a drizzle of honey.
- Lunch: Roasted Vegetable Wrap with baba ganoush and tahini sauce.
- Dinner: Lemon Herb Tofu with roasted Mediterranean vegetables.

Day 5:

- Breakfast: Overnight Oats with coconut milk, chia seeds, and mixed nuts.
- Lunch: Greek Quinoa Salad with olives, cherry tomatoes, and cucumbers.
- Dinner: Artichoke and Spinach Pasta with a creamy cashew sauce.

Day 6:
- Breakfast: Mediterranean Avocado Toast with cherry tomatoes and balsamic glaze.
- Lunch: Falafel Bowl with quinoa, roasted chickpeas, and tahini dressing.
- Dinner: Mushroom and Sun-Dried Tomato Risotto.

Day 7:

- Breakfast: Fruity Smoothie Bowl topped with fresh fruits and shredded coconut.
- Lunch: Grilled Vegetable Panini with vegan mozzarella and basil pesto.
- Dinner: Eggplant Rollatini with a tomato and basil sauce.

Day 8:
- Breakfast: Vegan French Toast with maple syrup and mixed berries.
- Lunch: Greek Cauliflower Rice Bowl with olives, cucumber, and tofu feta.
- Dinner: Mediterranean Stuffed Zucchini with bulgur wheat and herbs.

Day 9:
- Breakfast: Almond Butter and Banana Toast with a sprinkle of cinnamon.

- Lunch: Caprese Salad with vegan mozzarella, basil, and balsamic glaze.
- Dinner: Tomato and Lentil Stew with a side of crusty bread.

Day 10:
- Breakfast: Vegan Blueberry Muffins with a side of fresh fruit.
- Lunch: Hummus and Roasted Veggie Wrap with greens and pickled onions.
- Dinner: Greek Orzo Salad with cherry tomatoes, olives, and parsley.

Day 11:
- Breakfast: Berry Chia Smoothie with almond milk and hemp seeds.
- Lunch: Mediterranean Falafel Salad with a lemon-tahini dressing.

- Dinner: Lemon Herb Grilled Portobello Mushrooms.

Day 12:
- Breakfast: Tofu Scramble with spinach, tomatoes, and nutritional yeast.
- Lunch: Greek Pita Pockets with tomatoes, red onion, and vegan tzatziki.
- Dinner: Roasted Vegetable and Quinoa Buddha Bowl.

Day 13:
- Breakfast: Vegan Breakfast Burrito with black beans and avocado.
- Lunch: Mediterranean Lentil and Rice Stew with a squeeze of lemon.
- Dinner: Stuffed Tomatoes with rice, pine nuts, and fresh herbs.

Day 14:
- Breakfast: Vegan Banana Pancakes with maple syrup and sliced bananas.
- Lunch: Chickpea and Spinach Stew with a sprinkle of paprika.
- Dinner: Ratatouille with garlic bread on the side.

Day 15:
- Breakfast: Vegan Greek Yogurt Parfait with mixed berries and a drizzle of agave syrup.
- Lunch: Mediterranean Couscous Salad with cucumber, cherry tomatoes, and fresh mint.
- Dinner: Roasted Cauliflower with tahini sauce and pomegranate seeds.

Day 16:

- Breakfast: Green Smoothie with spinach, kale, banana, and almond milk.
- Lunch: Greek Chickpea Wraps with lettuce, tomatoes, and dairy-free Tzatziki.
- Dinner: Stuffed Bell Peppers with quinoa, black beans, and vegan cheese.

Day 17:
- Breakfast: Chia Seed Breakfast Bowl with coconut milk, mango, and toasted coconut flakes.
- Lunch: Falafel Mezze Platter with hummus, pickled vegetables, and pita bread.
- Dinner: Vegan Paella with artichokes, bell peppers, and green peas.

Day 18:

- Breakfast: Vegan Mediterranean Frittata with zucchini, red bell pepper, and Kalamata olives.

- Lunch: Greek Pasta Salad with cherry tomatoes, cucumber, and vegan feta.

- Dinner: Mushroom and Spinach Stuffed Tomatoes.

Day 19:

- Breakfast: Raspberry Coconut Overnight Oats with sliced almonds.

- Lunch: Mediterranean Lentil and Vegetable Soup with a side of crusty bread.

- Dinner: Vegan Moussaka with layers of eggplant, lentils, and béchamel sauce.

Day 20:

- Breakfast: Acai Smoothie Bowl with granola, fresh fruits, and shredded coconut.
- Lunch: Grilled Portobello Mushroom Sandwich with sun-dried tomato pesto.
- Dinner: Mediterranean Quinoa Stuffed Bell Peppers.

Day 21:
- Breakfast: Vegan Banana Walnut Muffins with a sprinkle of cinnamon.
- Lunch: Greek Rice Stuffed Peppers with tomatoes, onions, and olives.
- Dinner: Ratatouille Stuffed Zucchini Boats.

Day 22:
- Breakfast: Chocolate Chia Pudding with sliced strawberries and cacao nibs.

- Lunch: Greek Chickpea and Olive Pita Pockets with lettuce and red onion.
- Dinner: Lemon Herb Baked Tofu with roasted sweet potatoes.

Day 23:
- Breakfast: Mixed Berry Smoothie with almond milk and a handful of spinach.
- Lunch: Mediterranean Quinoa Salad with roasted vegetables and lemon dressing.
- Dinner: Vegan Spinach and Artichoke Dip with pita chips.

Day 24:
- Breakfast: Vegan Mediterranean Breakfast Burrito with roasted red peppers and avocado.

- Lunch: Greek Orzo and Spinach Salad with cherry tomatoes and cucumber.
- Dinner: Stuffed Eggplant Boats with couscous and raisins.

Day 25:
- Breakfast: Blueberry Almond Chia Seed Pudding with a drizzle of maple syrup.
- Lunch: Mediterranean Hummus Wrap with roasted eggplant and red bell pepper.
- Dinner: Roasted Vegetable and Lentil Bowl with a tahini dressing.

Day 26:
- Breakfast: Vegan Breakfast Tacos with black beans and avocado.

- Lunch: Greek Lentil Salad with cherry tomatoes, red onion, and fresh dill.
- Dinner: Quinoa-Stuffed Acorn Squash with dried cranberries and pumpkin seeds.

Day 27:
- Breakfast: Vegan Greek Yogurt with honey, pistachios, and pomegranate arils.
- Lunch: Falafel Salad with mixed greens, tomatoes, and cucumber.
- Dinner: Eggplant Involtini with a vegan ricotta filling.

Day 28:
- Breakfast: Mixed Berry Smoothie Bowl with coconut flakes and hemp seeds.

- Lunch: Mediterranean Couscous Stuffed Bell Peppers.
- Dinner: Vegan Spanakopita with a side of Greek Salad.

Day 29:
- Breakfast: Vegan Mediterranean Avocado Toast with cherry tomatoes and balsamic glaze.
- Lunch: Greek Chickpea and Vegetable Stew with a squeeze of lemon.
- Dinner: Mediterranean Cauliflower Rice with olives, artichokes, and pine nuts.

Day 30:
- Breakfast: Vegan Blueberry Pancakes with a dollop of almond butter.

- Lunch: Mediterranean Quinoa and Chickpea Bowl with lemon-tahini dressing.
- Dinner: Vegan Paella Stuffed Bell Peppers.

Remember to adapt this 30-day meal plan based on your dietary preferences and nutritional needs. Always make sure to include a variety of fruits, vegetables, legumes, and whole grains to enjoy the full benefits of a plant-based Mediterranean diet. Enjoy your culinary journey and embrace the delicious flavors of the Mediterranean!

Printed in Great Britain
by Amazon

38752300R00136